Proceedings of the Conference on Teaching Legal and Factual Research in Private Law Libraries

April 26 – April 29, 1990
Westfields International Conference Center
Chantilly, Virginia

Fred B. Rothman & Co.
Littleton, Colorado 80127
1991

Library of Congress Cataloging-in-Publication Data

Conference on Teaching Legal and Factual Research in Private Law Libraries (1990 : Westfield International Conference Center)

Proceedings of the Conference on Teaching Legal and Factual Research in Private Law Libraries : April 26-April 29, 1990, Westfield International Conference Center, Chantilly, Virginia.

p. cm.

Conference sponsored by Mead Data Central, Inc.

ISBN 0-8377-0911-3

1. Legal research–Study and teaching–United States–Congresses. 2. Law Libraries–United States–Congresses. I. Mead Data Central, Inc. II. Title.

KF240.C62 1991
340'.072073–dc20

91-17748
CIP

Printed in the United States of America

Acknowledgments

Mead Data Central, Inc. gratefully acknowledges the assistance and cooperation of the faculty, participants and Advisory Council for the 1990 Conference in Teaching Legal and Factual Research. Their dedication and enthusiasm to the editing and publication of the 1990 conference proceedings is greatly appreciated.

The following persons deserve a special acknowledgment. The 1990 Conference Council including Marie Wallace, Tory Trotta, Jim Hambleton, Marian Parker, Nick Finke, Suzanne Zumbro and Linda Couvion were the guiding lights that brought the conference to life. Also the work of Judy Vogel, Mike Krumm, Lisa Bear and Rhonda Raffel Fister is greatly appreciated for their creative and technical contributions to make these published proceedings a reality.

Finally, we would like to make a special acknowledgment in memory of Alan Holoch, Director of the Law Library and Professor of Law at Ohio State University. Alan was a faculty member on the panel discussion section Joint Ventures: Law School and Law Firms. Alan's enthusiasm and dynamic teaching style will be greatly missed by all.

Preface

In April 1990, Mead Data Central, Inc. sponsored a conference at the Westfields International Conference Center on the teaching legal and factual research in private law libraries. Mead Data Central annually sponsors the Graylyn Conference on teaching legal research in law libraries. The most recent Graylyn Conference faculty included private law librarians who saw the potential of a similar conference for private law librarians involved in teaching research.

The librarians that originally conceived of the program approached Mead Data Central to act as corporate sponsor, started the planning process, and put together the agenda. Due to the incredible efforts of the librarians on the Conference Council, the conference was a great success and planned in a very short time frame. The five basic areas addressed were: presentation skills; teaching options; modifying content for different audience; cooperating with law schools; and working with in–house professional development programs.

The program format was varied to maximize learning and sharing of information. There were structured breakout sessions, lectures, videotaping and much sharing of ideas by the approximately 25 faculty and 35 attendees.

Table of Contents

Page

Introduction

Marie Wallace

We are going to experience an unusual amount of involvement at this Conference. I am glad to welcome you all here this evening and to begin to involve you in what is going to be a thumbs up conference. It is really remarkable that it is taking place as the idea for a conference on teaching legal and factual research for private law librarians was conceived less than six months ago. Let me take a few minutes to give you a bit of conference background and to introduce to you some of the key players.

The idea for the Westfields Conference began last November at the Graylyn Conference, a Mead–sponsored conference for teaching legal research in law schools. Three firm librarians were invited to participate as faculty and were very impressed with the format, pace and substance of the program. It was one fantastic conference because it was small, relevant and gave us a clear understanding of why summer and fall associates arrive at firms with limited research skills. We wanted to extend the Graylyn conference concept to a larger audience of private librarians, to build on law school programs, to promote joint ventures and to support the instruction programs already operative in firm libraries. So we put our thinking hats on.

These three private librarians were Barbara Geier, Tory Trotta and myself. Because we had attended Graylyn together, we had a very clear vision of a program for private librarians. We recognized that most private librarians already teach research on a one–on–one basis but many do not have the presentation skills or confidence to develop larger, more formal research programs. Many are unaware of the teaching options and resource materials available and need more information on presentation skills, training models and instruction tools. You should understand that when the three of us left Graylyn, we were zealots.

We approached Nick Finke at Mead with the idea of a companion conference to Graylyn Conference. Nick had been at Graylyn and understood the context of our zeal and enthusiasm. Fortunately, he was also in a position to effect a decision.

Before we knew it, Mead agreed to sponsor a conference, an Advisory Council was created and members of the Council convened here at Westfields during the last week in January to turn the idea into a program agenda. As you can appreciate from the time frame, the program was implemented very rapidly but this may be the norm. You need to know how to put together a program quickly as chances are you will not have much notice. A decision maker may come to you with the idea of doing or expanding a research program. You acquiesce because you have been here at Westfields and he or she says, "Fine, how about Tuesday?" I notice that you all are chuckling. Perhaps you are familiar with this scenario.

This program is designed to present you with a better understanding of the private research context. One of the things we learned at Graylyn was that research in firms is client driven and includes extensive factual research skills. This contrasts with research in law schools which is case driven and limited to legal research skills.

Further, it is very difficult to generalize about specific research programs for practicing lawyers. Law practices are unique and differ so much that programs almost have to be tailored to each setting. One firm will need federal income tax research training while others may find trademark or labor research essential.

Before I introduce the people who put this conference together, let me note that when this program was planned and the date selected, we were unaware that it was National Library Week. I think it is particularly fitting that we serendipitously picked a date to correspond with national recognition of what librarians do.

The Advisory Council was selected with the aim of maintaining a close connection to AALL and the PLL–SIS, designating a broad geographic representation, keeping the Council small and selecting people with strong program planning experience. In addition to myself as Chair of the Advisory Council, members of the Advisory Council are:

- Barbara Geier, Director of Information Services, Powell, Goldstein, Frazer & Murphy, Atlanta. Barbara is chair of the in–house training module.
- Tory Trotta, Law Librarian, Lewis and Roca, Phoenix. Tory is chair of the joint venture module.

- Marian Parker, Manager, Mead Data Central, Dayton. Marian provided the Council with reality checks.
- Nick Finke, Director of Large Law Firm Market, Mead Data Central, Dayton. Nick is the controller of finances.
- Susanne Zumbro, Librarian, Piper & Marbury, Washington, D.C. Susanne coordinated the selection of applicants.
- James Hambleton, Manager of Legal Information Resources, Haynes and Boone, Dallas. Jim is chair of the defining the audience module.
- Gitelle Seer, Directory of Library Services, Dewey, Ballentine, Busby, Palmer & Wood, New York. Gitelle is chair of the options for teaching research module.
- Linda Couvion, Manager, Mead Data Central, Dayton. Linda selected the conference site and coordinated food, travel and lodging arrangements.
- Lisa Bear, Mead Data Central. Lisa functioned as a behind–the–scenes conference planner and was particularly helpful to me in assembling the Presentation Skills handout.

The Advisory Council has done an outstanding job. I would like to acknowledge their work and want to add that in addition to providing the financial support for this conference, MDC has given the Advisory Council strong intellectual support contributing ideas, suggestions and critiques.

Now I would like to introduce Nick Finke, Director of Large Law Firm Market, MDC to say a few words about the sponsorship of the Conference.

Nick Finke

Thank you very much, Marie. I'm here to welcome you on behalf of Mead Data Central. We at Mead Data are very happy to be able to sponsor a conference like this. As you may have noticed, this conference is not focused on computer–assisted legal research, or, indeed, on anything to do with computers, but rather on legal research in general. The reason for this is that we really believe that by empowering you to the greatest degree, we can to further the cause of legal research, we cannot help but win.

Nick Finke

As I was listening to Marie, I couldn't help but reflect on the Graylyn conference. The two things about Graylyn that made it so special and so successful were that it was small and intensely relevant. As you can tell from the size of this room, we are certainly a small group. With the outstanding people both on the faculty and among those attending, we cannot be anything but relevant. With these two things going for us, I'm sure this is going to be an outstanding conference. Thank you all for coming.

Keynote Address

The Electronic Media and the Transformation of the Law

Ethan Katsh

I am really very honored to open this conference for you. To Marie Wallace, to Nick Finke, Lisa Bear, Linda Couvion and others of you who planned this event, I am quite grateful to you.

Nick called me in January and asked me to be the keynote speaker for you this evening and I was very flattered. But I must tell you that I was also quite relieved to look in the program and see that I am listed as providing opening remarks and not as the keynoter for the conference. I say this because a few days after my phone conversation with Nick, I started to feel a little troubled about the invitation. There was something bothering me. I kept having this nagging, recurring thought about being a keynote speaker and it took me a little while before I realized what was happening. I finally became aware that the source of my anxiety was very simple. It was that the word "keynote" sounded as if it were a contraction of "key number" and "headnote." If you were to merge "key number" and "headnote," keynote is what you would get. Well, I hope you get the picture. Here, Mead has been kind enough to bring us together and I kept having images of Mead's main competitor.

But this wasn't even the worst of it. I mentioned the invitation to a colleague who teaches copyright law and he told me that Nick had actually put me in some legal jeopardy. A basic principle of copyright law, and you probably know this since these days all librarians have become experts in copyright law, is that the copyright owner owns all derivative works. The legal reasoning was as follows: if West owns the key numbers and owns the headnotes, they must also own the keynotes. This made me even more anxious. My anxieties were beginning to get the better of me, but the lawyer in me took over and I figured this problem was just in my mind. I said to myself nobody ever would use keynote in this way, as a contraction for headnote and key number, and it didn't even make any sense to use it this way, so I couldn't be in any trouble.

In the old days, I would have stopped here and, in a short time, would have wondered why I had wasted any time on such foolish thoughts. But these aren't the old days. The new times are here. LEXIS® is here. And my obsessive side took over again. And I dialed up LEXIS, typed in the word keynote and, as the letters scrolled across the page, I began to get that sinking feeling any lawyer gets when he or she finds an "unwelcome precedent." I was presented with the case of *International Shipping Co. v. Hydra Offshore Inc.*, 675 F. Supp. 146, in which Judge Leisure of the Southern District of New York uses keynote in just the manner I described. Well, I won't continue with this any longer. If, by bestowing upon me the honor of opening the conference, you have also made me into a copyright violation, I am indeed flattered. On the other hand, I suggest Nick, that you inform your lawyers that there might be a conspiracy afoot to secure control over everything that has to do with keys and notes.

More seriously, I think that Mead deserves some credit for bringing us here. While LEXIS and other databases are indeed quite miraculous, the development of electronic databases has also made your job, or some aspects of your job, much more difficult. I hope that it has also made your work more interesting. I get the impression that librarian, as a generic description of who you are, is less meaningful than it once was. Some of you have acquired some new roles and titles. I don't know if you get paid any more than you did, but half of you are listed as having titles that probably did not exist five or ten years ago. I hope that you have also acquired some new respect. But what is perhaps going on in your profession is also going on in the legal profession. I will come back to this again in a few minutes, but I think that one of the things you may be feeling about your profession and one of the things you need to recognize about the lawyers who employ you is that there is a process of professional fragmentation occurring. Just what a lawyer is and what all lawyers have in common with each other, and how they are different from others are serious, difficult, but I think also unavoidable questions. We still call them lawyers, but the thread that binds them is being loosened, and I think that you have to be aware of that.

From my point of view, changes in how we communicate are contributing to all of this and I hope that I can provide some perspective and background to the issues that have brought you here and have brought some stress to your lives.

On the subject of personal stress, I was once told of a person who was feeling depressed and anxious and nervous and consulted a psychiatrist about his problem. To get a handle on what was the source of the patient's problem, the psychiatrist decided that he would give the patient a Rorschach test, an inkblot test.

The psychiatrist pulled out his box of inkblots, held up the first one and asked, "Mr. Smith, what do you see in this picture?

Smith took a look at it and said "That's easy. That's a picture of two people making love."

The psychiatrist took out a second inkblot and said "Mr. Smith, what do see in this one?"

"Same thing. Two people making love." This went on for some time, with the patient seeing the same thing no matter what shape picture he was shown. Finally, the psychiatrist stopped, put down his box of inkblots, and said "Mr. Smith, you may not like my diagnosis, but I think that you have an unhealthy fixation with sex."

Smith seemed a little shocked but reacted quickly, "That may be true, but can I ask you a question. Why do you have so many dirty pictures?"

I thought I would take the risk this evening of discussing with you my fixation, my way of looking at the law, what I see when I examine what law is and how it works. My fixation is not sex or dirty pictures. That would probably make a more entertaining or lively discussion. Maybe that is what some of you see in the law. But my own fixation is on something different. It concerns the role of communication and information in the law. When I look at law, I see not the lawyers and not the judges, not the law firm offices or courthouses, but a communicative process, one in which the flow of information and the reliance on means of communications is fundamentally important. We are in a developmental or transition period in which new tools of transmitting, storing, organizing and processing information are fairly quickly replacing more traditional methods. I think this has very important consequences for the law and for persons involved in working with lawyers. Certainly, there are consequences for persons doing legal training and research. I would like to persuade you to see things my way, to see the things I am seeing. Obviously, I think that I am unlike the patient because what I am seeing is really there. But then again, the patient also thought that.

Ethan Katsh

I would like to talk in a general way about what I think is involved for you and for the law in shifting from a reliance on print to a reliance on electronic forms of communication. I think that there is a context for approaching this new relationship we have with electronic information sources. And I would like to devote a little time to some of the practical concerns that have motivated you to come here for this conference.

Let me begin with a few words about how my book evolved and about my approach to the subject. The book is really as much about the past as it is about the future, and I think my remarks will be as well. If electronic forms of communication are joining or replacing print, which is what I think is the fundamental change taking place, and if the law has been dependent upon print for some time, and I think that this is also true, then I think it important to understand why this has been so. And I think that history does provide some answers for us.

I hope what I say will have some relevance to the present, because you are here because of pressing problems, common problems, that are making your jobs difficult. There are some things I am optimistic about, where I think things will improve for you, and there are also some things I am pessimistic about, in the sense that the challenges and obstacles facing you may increase. There is, in other words, good news and bad news. But I also feel quite strongly we should not focus exclusively on the present. The present, the status quo, has a shorter life span than it used to have. The present is not with us for as long as it used to be. This is an era of rapid change and one of the reasons change is accelerated is because new technologies allow new information to replace old information much more quickly than it did in the past. Part of the challenge we all face is that we must confront our problems and also adapt to change, learn how to cope with it and recognize it as a feature of modern life. I think that we are helped in this regard when we have a context for discussions about the present. No one has ever had the technologies we have but others have experienced some of the challenges we face and history does provide us with some insights that might be helpful for us.

My own interest in communications technology developed, at least partly, out of an interest in a variety of technological developments that had captured public attention. And all new technologies have an impact on the law. The automobile has had a strong impact on torts law. Medical and biological discoveries have generated a need for new legal doctrines. Nuclear technology has earth–shattering or earth–ending potential which law may be called upon to deal with. I think that such technologies raise a host of important and interesting challenges for lawyers and law schools.

I gradually came to believe, however, that communications technologies were different in a very significant way. The technologies I just mentioned are primarily a challenge to discrete areas of legal doctrine. Information technology, I believe, is different. It is different because the potential exists for many many facets of law to be affected. I think it is different because, as I view it, the law runs on information. Much of the legal process is the communication of information. All of law is not affected by the automobile because law is not composed of automobiles. But law is, in almost all of its parts, dependent on communication and information.

If you thought about it for a little while, I am sure that you could generate a list of ways in which you see information and communication touching the goals, processes, concepts and institutions of law. And I would be curious later to hear some of these. My book represents my own list, and let me give you a few examples of what I mean.

One of the clearest and perhaps most fundamental examples is precedent, which involves using a body of information in a particular way. A process of precedent requires that there be a means for storing, accessing and organizing information. Legal reasoning implies that there is some information categorized as legal and that those trained in the law use this information in a special way. Trial procedure is a process for admitting and excluding information. Both judicial and jury decisions involve the evaluation of information. The legal profession itself may be viewed as an occupational group that has, for better or for worse, secured control over some body of information. In general, manipulation of information underlies the way legal institutions work, how legal doctrines are applied and how social and moral values are translated into legal values.

Much of this is, I think, relatively obvious, namely that the law and people involved in the law will inevitably have a close relationship with information. If any of you have gone to law school, you know that much of legal training consists of structuring and nurturing this relationship with information. Law has a knowledge component and an action component and the law assumes that the actions we take are driven by the knowledge we have about law, are consistent with the knowledge component. Those participating in the legal process, namely lawyers, need training because most humans do not use information, or at least legal information, as lawyers do. There are obviously actions taken that are inconsistent with what our minds know and actions that are taken in the absence of legal knowledge. All I am saying is that the law is one of those knowledge systems or information systems, that, in theory at least, is supposed to be principled and rational rather than emotional or intuitive. And in order for law to work according to this model at all, it must rely quite heavily on some medium to organize, store and communicate that information.

As I thought about this, I realized that there were three areas that I wanted to look at that might help me determine how and why a new information technology might bring about change.

First, it seemed to me that if the shift from print media to electronic media had implications for law, I reasoned that important changes must have taken place centuries ago when print established itself. I thought that I should find out where the law had been most receptive to print several hundred years ago. Where it had been quick to change then, it might also be vulnerable to change now. My concern was not, at least at that time, with legal doctrines but with methods, with institutions, with concepts, even values.

If this period did turn out to be a significant one, the second thing I was interested in was why. What special qualities did print possess that made it an agent for change? Why were the differences between print and writing significant?

Third, I felt that I needed to understand, in a similar way, how the electronic media, principally computers and television, differed from print. I assumed that if I could identify areas of law that were linked in some way to qualities of print, these areas would change as information in electronic form replaced print.

What I sensed was less important than any of this, and what I decided to resist looking at as long as I could was how the new technologies were being employed or who was using them. I was determined not to extrapolate from what was currently going on. Or at least to resist doing this because that approach seemed misguided in a number of ways I shall mention in a few moments.

In any event, the historical period after Gutenberg proved to be an extremely rewarding period to study. It seemed to me that there were numerous parallels between that period and our own and some potentially important lessons for us. Let me give you one example:

In the early years after Gutenberg, during which printing spread very rapidly, it was welcomed by the powerful institutions of that time, just as computers have been welcomed today. One of the institutions that welcomed the technology most eagerly was the Church. The Church was still, in the 1400s, the most powerful European institution, and various church officials stated that printing was a God–given gift. Some monasteries took up printing, and the largest category of books printed before fifteen hundred were religious. It was not coincidental that Gutenberg had chosen the Bible as the first book he would print. That seemed to be a shrewd economic evaluation of his potential market, but in fact he had trouble selling them. In any event, if one looked at what was being printed, at content, one would have jumped to the conclusion that the Church was correct in its analysis and that the new technology would enhance its power and authority.

But looking at content alone would have been a great error. Printing had brought with it other changes. Any new information technology does a variety of things in addition to carrying information. We get a distorted impression of the effect of a new medium if we only look at who is using the new technology at a particular point in time, and how. What the Church didn't understand and what is still not generally understood is that we can be seriously misled if we look simply at what information is being moved from someone to someone else.

Thus, it was not a coincidence that the most momentous challenge to the medieval Church occurred shortly after the development of printing. The Protestant Reformation would not have occurred as it did without the invention of moveable type. In 1519, Martin Luther tacked his complaints about the Catholic church to a church door in Wittenberg, Germany. More significantly, however, his Ninety Five Theses were printed and circulated widely. It has been estimated that in the three years following his historic act, more than three hundred thousand copies of Luther's writings were sold. His translation of the Bible sold even more copies and further helped his cause.

I am generally skeptical that a new medium will simply enhance the power of an existing institution that is able to afford to employ it. The reason for this is that the status quo is dominated by institutions that have been able to exploit successfully the existing medium. If the qualities of the old medium are, somehow, deeply embedded in the practices of this institution, it will have to change quite quickly and radically to be able to adapt to and exploit the new medium because the new medium probably has very different strengths and qualities.

Thus, any institution that had been successful because of control over the written word was faced with a whole variety of challenges. Print, we should recall, brought a whole series of changes. There was mass production, the ability to reach many. There was also what some consider print's most significant feature, standardization, the fact that all copies were now uniform. All of this contributed to the growth of your profession and to the growth of the legal profession. There were now more books, authoritative books, and books that were more useable than manuscripts. Printed books began to look like modern books, rather than like some student's notebook, which was what manuscripts often looked like. Printed works were more useable because, for the first time, books had indexes, clear page numbers and a title page. One could easily tell who had written a book. Spelling was gradually standardized. These new styles of organization and appearance provided a common frame of reference for readers. Uniform editions allowed comparisons to be made among related works and for research findings to be published. The point is that there was a lot more information and it was necessary to organize the growing body of knowledge. Clearer boundary lines were established separating areas of knowledge. Those interested in law could focus more clearly on what was legal in nature and what was not.

The growth of libraries and the growth of specialized libraries obviously contributed to this. Fifteen to twenty volumes had been an impressive personal library in 1500. A lawyer at that time with a large library might have had thirty–five volumes and most of these would have been religious or non–legal in nature. The library at Cambridge in the fifteenth century had only five hundred books. But by 1550, personal collections of five hundred volumes were not uncommon. Perhaps more important, while most libraries were religious in nature in the late fifteenth century, by the early fifteen hundreds most were secular. Thus, while there were certainly more Bibles in circulation, there were also more books of a secular nature. Control of the press, in spite of some efforts by the Church, turned out to be incredibly difficult. To the extent that the Church had benefited from the limitations of writing, it was bound to have major problems in the new communications environment.

The outcome of all this, I believe, was the development of institutions that exploited the powers of print. And law, I think, was one of these. Printing was introduced into England in 1476. Five years later the first law books were printed, and in 1485 the printing of parliamentary session laws began. The year book period ended in 1535, and two years later the first printed reports of cases appeared.

A famous architect once said that form follows function. The history of precedent is that function followed form. One couldn't have a system of binding precedent if one couldn't find prior cases or if there were different conflicting versions of prior cases or if one didn't trust writing generally. It is quite clear to me that the printing of reports led to a clear change in the legal authority of a report of a judge's ruling. So much so that by 1765, Lord Campbell could state, "If it is law, it will be found in our books. If it is not to be found there, it is not law." Prior to printing, it is inconceivable that a judge would have thought in this way.

That law was an area of great activity for printers was important not only because there was now a lot more law available, but because this law was now in books, in printed books. It was, for the first time, contained in a medium that had great storage capacity, that was reliable and trustworthy, that could provide a tangible identity to an abstract idea. If law was gradually recognized to be autonomous and independently powerful, if it was thought that there could be a unified profession just as there was an organized and systematic body of law, then I think that printing contributed greatly toward this.

I would be happy to discuss print further later if anyone wishes. But let me move on and outline some qualities of electronic media. Most people, I think, are initially impressed with computers because they view them as more powerful technologies than print. Doing the same task, computers can do more or do the same thing faster. For example, computers can store more information in a smaller space than books. Writing, revising, editing on computers can take place more quickly. One can obviously find more cases more quickly using LEXIS than using traditional materials. This is true, but I would urge that, in addition to being awestruck by these great capabilities, we pay some attention to the subtle qualities and recognize how these technologies do what they do, and not simply look at what they do. Particularly since Orwell provided us with the powerful image of Big Brother, we have assumed that control of information would be facilitated by our new technologies. I am highly skeptical about this. Indeed, it seems to me much more likely that we or our institutions, such as law, which have grown because of their ability to control information in a particular way, may have problems as this becomes more difficult to do.

I suggested before that printed texts could be thought of as being self–contained, tangible, reliable, authoritative and complete. Can we say this about electronic works? I am not so sure. A printed work and an electronic work may have similar content, the same words, but the electronic work will be organized differently, access will be different, it will be revised more often, and new tools for processing data will be available. And if, as a result, our attitude toward information changes, then our approach to law, which is information and which is largely printed information, may change as well.

This suggests three things to me. The first is that we understand that institutions will be changing. One of the institutions that may be changing in front of your very eyes is the law firm. My feeling is that you are in the vanguard, that you are working in the legal arena where change will occur faster than anywhere else. I say this assuming that large law firms are using electronic information sources more than most other practitioners. I suspect that you use electronic databases as much as anyone and perhaps more than anyone. Marie sent me a list of databases that are used at O'Melveny Myers. I work at an institution that takes pride in having one of the top fifty research libraries, but I don't think that we have the capabilities that she has. We have access to more books than you do, but we do not have as much access to that world of electronic information.

I know that Marie finds that it is problematic to have access to so much without knowing all the time what it is she has access to. What I would say is that expanded access is a technology–driven phenomenon. Computers are communicative devices and we are witnessing the linking together in a network of previously independent and isolated databases. It seems to me that it is, in a sense, unnatural for an electronic library to be separate and unconnected to other electronic sources of information. To keep Westlaw or LEXIS unconnected to the vast and growing number of law–related or even non–legal sources of electronic information is to use the technology in an inefficient manner. What I mean is that since computers are communicative technologies, it is inefficient not to have them linked to all other sources of available information.

It is interesting to me that law school libraries are the prototypical example of collections that have been self-contained and traditionally separate from other university collections. Electronic media break down spatial barriers. That is one of their greatest powers. The lawyer at the terminal is really as close to any non-legal data base as he or she is to LEXIS, unless you consciously decide to erect some barrier, in which case I think you will run into other problems. In other words, for the user not to be able to do something because the medium has limited powers is one thing. There is not much we can do about this and the user will not feel too frustrated. To impose a restriction on a medium that has such capabilities is, in a way, censorship and will evoke different responses.

LEXIS and Westlaw know this and have already expanded greatly from their limited beginnings. Compare the history of print and electronic law collections. The history of the printed law library is growth from very small general collections into these large distinctly legal collections that are found in many law schools. The growth of Westlaw and LEXIS, in a sense, is just the opposite. They began as legal collections and are growing larger and more general, with more and easier access to non-legal material.

It seems to me that law in the books is really more than a phrase or symbol. We are provided with tangible representation of something abstract, something that we can point to as authoritative. Electronic information is considered intangible. Electronic libraries can store huge amounts of data, but I doubt that they can provide the same feeling of separateness, of autonomous existence, that print collections now do. Your print collection is self-contained. If I keep walking in the print law library, I will eventually bump into a wall. And I will know that that is where the law collection ends. Electronic libraries can lead me from source to source to source almost forever.

I think that all of this has implications for law firms and for the legal profession. The profession is, after all, a monopoly, controlling a body of information, and not eager to allow others access to what it controls. If this were to happen, and control over the body of legal knowledge were to begin to diminish, the profession would gradually lose its distinctiveness and its character would change. If you find yourself thinking frequently that you know as much as the lawyers know, then the line separating the profession from others may be beginning to evaporate.

The other two areas that I look at with interest concern individuals. The first of these concerns the new skills that are needed to become electronically literate. Securing electronic information makes demands on those of us who were brought up in a completely non–electronic environment. Fairly intelligent and successful people discover that there is something out there about which they are completely ignorant. I know that the incompetence or ineptness or lack of expertise many of you encounter in your firms is one of the main reasons you are here. I sympathize with you, but I also confess that I am somewhat hopeful about this, at least as far as the learning of skills is concerned. As I looked at the program for the next three days, I was impressed with the planning that has gone into the conference and I am certain that you will leave here feeling more confident about your ability to assist others.

But I am also hopeful because I think that the technology and the programmers will help us. Or at least they should. I think that some of the problems you face are due to the stage we are now in. I call the stage we are in a clumsy stage. My point is not simply that there are lots of the uninitiated out there and that they will gradually be reduced in number, but that the means we are now using to get information will probably look primitive in three, five or ten years. I don't know if you can hold out that long, but that is another problem.

Let me frame what I am saying this way. If you have problems with poorly trained lawyers, with lawyers who are unaware of what information can be accessed with their fingertips, I think the situation will improve no matter how much more vast and more varied the world of electronically available information becomes. The level of skill in using communications software is probably no worse today than the level of skill was in using word processing software five years ago. But my main point is that we can be helped enormously if, in addition to conferences such as this that focus on how to teach the skills, the software improves so that learning becomes easier and quicker and, most importantly, more interesting. I would hope that the people here from Mead would be receptive to hearing from you over the next few days if you have suggestions about how software might be improved.

My perspective on how to improve the skill to navigate in the world of electronic databases is that it is a little like the issue of automobile safety. I think car manufacturers have learned that safer driving comes from providing safer cars as well as teaching drivers to be more conscientious. Automobile safety does not only come from better drivers. Car manufacturers should compete with each other by producing safer cars and we should drive more carefully.

The relevance of this to this weekend, and I hope that our hosts perceive this suggestion as advice that is helpful rather than ungracious, is that you should communicate your feeling about how communications software and interfaces with data can be improved. We should have better software, interfaces that help us out more than what we have now does. Another way of saying this is that I would like to see database providers competing not simply in terms of quantity, how much is available, how much is being added each month, and so forth, but in terms of quality and ease of use. And that is partly up to you.

I think that this is important because of the other impact on the individual who is faced with using new techniques of research and sources of information. There is the skill problem, about which I have just spoken and about which you are very knowledgeable, and then there is what I would call the cultural problem. In my mind, the problem you face is not simply one of teaching new skills. Entering the electronic world is difficult not only because novices find it difficult to get what they want, because they lack skills, but also because it is disorienting. The electronic world challenges habits of thought that have been developed over a long period of time. And this problem remains even though you teach someone some skills and how to navigate through some database. Frankly, I myself still feel disoriented in dealing with this other culture, because that is what I think it is. Its language is not the same and the habits of thought that are required to be successful are different from what they are in print. It is a culture that has a lot of appeal to me but it expects and assumes some different things than does the print culture, and it will take me some time to get used to it if I do decide to move there.

It is not as easy to explain this as it is to talk about skills, but let me give you one illustration. Why has word processing been so successful? Most lawyers seem to be able to adapt to word processing not only because it does the job more quickly than a typewriter. There is something more. I think this extra dimension is that whenever the user starts feeling uncomfortable, he or she can get their equilibrium restored by a very simple mechanism. They can print out whatever they were working on and work or edit the words on paper. I look at the ability to print out copy and to edit paper copy as the equivalent of going back to the womb or sucking one's thumb. Users can return to the print culture for a few moments whenever they wish. It is anxiety reducing. I don't think that word processing would have spread as quickly as it has, with all of the extraordinary benefits it provides, if all editing and reading had to be done on screen and paper copies could not be made.

Maybe I am wrong about this but, if I can take a moment longer, you might consider your colleagues who send you memos that look as if they were printed. There is an incredible amount of material flowing around institutions that uses traditional typefaces, justified margins and looks as if it had been sent out to a printer. What is the appeal of this?

I think that it is interesting that something very similar happened once before. The first printed books, for example, looked very much like manuscripts. The typeface used was similar to a written script. Gutenberg's 42–line Bible was printed in a letter–type which faithfully reproduced a familiar handwritten script. That this could be done was proof of the greatness of the typesetter. It was an economically wise decision and also a psychologically comforting decision that helped guarantee the acceptance of print. And we are witnessing something similar, I think. It took a little time for the typefaces we are accustomed to to develop and I think that as we become used to the electronic culture, we will also develop more novel forms of presentation. For now, however, I think that one of the sources of resistance is that some of the cultural guideposts are missing for persons brought up in a print environment. The technology has simply changed faster than the culture.

I have no excuse for the lawyers you encounter who have poor research skills with traditional materials. They lack necessary skills in spite of the fact that they have spent many hours with books, in libraries, in bookstores. They are already turned on to books and know what books are like. They are part of the print culture. I am more sympathetic to the person coming to you for instruction or guidance in using an electronic database. You are not, with this person, building upon fifteen to twenty years of familiarity of looking at print.

What does this tell me about the future, say five or ten years from now? It leads me to think that with some help from the technology, and if it becomes more economical to do so, that you may be complaining that you have people in your firms who take up too much of your time talking about this database or that database. But I also wonder who these people will be and what it is they will be doing.

In any event, I think that an era of new communications technologies and an explosion of data and of forms for presenting data provide you with interesting challenges. This is a period of rapid change, of growing complexity, of new forms of organization, of new relationships, and of increasing conflict as these relationships encounter problems. Lawyers should benefit from a lot of this. But legal knowledge is also being altered, and I wonder about how a lawyer will be defined in this new environment as the knowledge base underlying the occupation is transformed.

You are right in the middle of this. Your jobs are certainly not easier than they were, but I think they are more interesting. And if you keep your eyes open and are sensitive to the powers of the new technologies, I think that you will continue to have a fascinating vantage point to see why and how the law is changing.

Presentation Skills

Marie Wallace

The Advisory Council planned this Conference using state–of–the–art presentation techniques so that you as participants would *experience* a good program at the same time you were learning how to create one. Let me highlight some of the techniques you have experienced so far.

This Conference began before you arrived at Westfields prepared to be videotaped. It actually began for you as you completed the application to attend. Remember all those questions in addition to your name and address? Those questions were a form of "gap" analysis. In order to plan an effective program, it is necessary to determine what attendees already know and what skills they need to acquire to do a particular task. The "gap" between present skills and needed skills is what training programs are designed to cover.

Last night we used the icebreaker technique at dinner. This is a subtle technique that is often used at the beginning of training programs to make people feel comfortable and to bond them into a working group.

Did you notice this morning that breakfast was a buffet? Individual selection is an adult education technique. A buffet gives participants control and choice over the eating agenda.

Seating arrangements are another important aspect of presentations. The ideal seating arrangement for a small training group is around a table. For a larger group, large tables positioned in a "U" shape is excellent. This layout makes it possible for the presenter to walk in among the group.

The "U" arrangement was requested for the Presentation Skills module. Unfortunately, the Conference Center misunderstood the request and we were provided the auditorium. During the remaining modules, you will experience a variety of other types of seating. Please notice how the physical layout changes the feel of a presentation as the conference progresses.

Where we are now, in an auditorium, is very formal. Spatially, it says to the audience "classroom." This often makes adults feel passive, as if they were back in the third grade. If you want to involve adults, you want to be cautious about reminding them of being children again.

Let me draw your attention to the posters on the wall. These are reproduced in the Presentation Skills handbook so you do not have to copy them. They are another means of involving you with presentation skills information. We live in an age of visual messages. Graphics are an important method of information transfer.

In attempting to surround you with presentation skills information, I tried to arrange with the Westfields Conference Center to put subliminal messages on your TV last night. I don't think it worked. Did anyone get a message about Presentation Skills off the TV last night?

There will be a resource table outside each meeting room. The materials displayed on the resource table are for you to look at — not to take. There are many items of interest where we had only a single sample and are making them available to you this way. For instance, all the articles in my Presentation Skills Bibliography are on the resource table.

The Presentation Skills module consists then of an infra-structure which includes:

- Gap analysis
- Icebreakers
- Lesson plan based on adult education theory
  - Learner is self-directing
  - Specific goals
  - Practical answers for today's problems
- Variety of training methods
  - Videos
  - Demonstration
  - Lecture
  - Panels
  - Discussion groups
  - Outing
- Facilitative techniques
  - Seating arrangements
  - Resource table
  - Visuals

Handouts
Feedback
Summation
Evaluation of the program

Most of us associate lectures with clock–watching college experiences. I recall only five really excellent lecturers in all my college years, including graduate school. Does that mean the lecture method is no good? Certainly not. It is more a reflection of the priorities at the University of California. The lecture circuit is alive and well. Good lecturers are paid handsomely and are in great demand. Properly used and appropriately applied, the lecture method remains one of the best means of information transfer.

All the Presentation Skills materials are in the handout which has been so nicely spiral bound and tabbed by MDC [see Appendix]. Please turn to the Preface. There you will find the goals of the Presentation Skills module:

1. Recognize the difference between teaching and training.
2. Conduct a gap analysis of their own presentation skills.
3. Apply adult learning principles to build their skills.
4. Discover their own style of humor.
5. Use the lecture method effectively.
6. Identify the critical components of training programs.

Whenever you plan a program, you should have specific goals in mind and make the goals clear to the audience. Ann mentioned this as part of lecturing effectively. The goals for the Presentation Skills module of this Conference are focused on how you can develop and improve your presentation skills.

Certainly, you are not going to be able to come away from Westfields an instantly improved presenter, but you will know how to build on your existing skills. Learning to communicate ideas to others is like learning to play tennis. It may take two years of practice with supervised instruction to become proficient and for you to feel comfortable on the court. The materials in the handout provide a path for you. You must set your own goals. This is a form of contract learning which is described in one of the articles in the bibliography. The Presentations Skills handout will reinforce what you learn here, provide you with a gestalt and serve as a reference (pathfinder) as you plan programs.

The first tab in the Presentation Skills handout is "Differences Between Speakers and Trainers." In my opinion, a training model is more appropriate for private law librarians than the teaching model. What is the difference?

The teaching model is what you usually encounter in school. Concentration is on the subject. You take a class in economics, or we are going to study geography. The teaching model focuses on and is organized by what the instructor knows about the subject. The audience passively receives the prepackaged information.

By contrast, the training model concentrates on the trainee. What does the already trainee know? What skills does the trainee need to acquire to perform a particular job? Training takes up where education stops. It is designed to develop practical skills instead of imparting broad knowledge.

What you are trying to do in the training model is to modify performance behavior. You, as the trainer, have a subdued role as facilitator. The audience should actively mold the training agenda to their particular needs. You need to involve trainees as soon as possible to signal that this is their training session. This is why the icebreaker technique was introduced last night and why I spoke of "involvement" during the welcome. Both are messages to you that this is a training, not a teaching, model.

The difference between the teaching and training models is epitomized in the poster on the wall and in your handout, "Effective Use of Visual Aids." People retain 20% of what they hear, 50% of what they hear and see, and 70% of what they hear, see and do. The degree of audience involvement makes a great deal of difference as to how much information is retained and whether it can be applied immediately to a problem.

How do you get trainees involved? You might want to use the *Encyclopedia of Icebreakers* or the *Encyclopedia of Group Activities,* both mentioned in my bibliography and both at the resource table. These two publications are filled with suggestions and may spark your own ideas.

Let's suppose that you are going to do a session on securities or factual research in your firm. At the beginning of the presentation, there will be a short time when people come into the room and have nothing to grab their interest. A well–designed icebreaker, such as a trivia quiz on your firm or city, can provide transitional activity. If your session were on securities research, the quiz could be on how to select a stock broker. Or if the session is on factual research, the trivia quiz might be on locating good or cheap local restaurants.

Earlier I mentioned the "gap" analysis. I was talking to Ellen Callinan during the break and was reminded that her article in the current issue of *Law Library Journal* (v. 82, p. 39, Winter 1990) includes a survey. She uses this questionnaire at her firm to determine what training is needed. This is her "gap" analysis.

It is essential that you determine in advance what your target audience needs to know. You cannot identify a group and effectively train them if they have different backgrounds, levels of expertise or kinds of practices. Training programs must differentiate the needs of individual groups and respond accordingly.

There are many articles in my bibliography that cover the concept of training. I suggest you read some of these, or others easily found in management literature, and seriously consider the training model over the teaching model when you implement research programs.

Many of the articles about in–house training written by lawyers fail to distinguish between these two models of instruction. Principles of training are more commonly understood by the management of large corporations than by the management of law firms. In–house training is only beginning to be accepted as a economic necessity by lawyers.

The second tab in the Presentation Skills handout is the "Bibliography." It begins with a list of associations to join. People cannot learn presentation skills by just reading about them. These skills are complex physical/intellectual activities. They are learned through practice and challenge. Associations provide these opportunities.

I recommend joining Toastmasters' because I am familiar with its program. My chapter meets once a week for one hour at noon and provides many different and fun kinds of speaking and program planning opportunities. It also brings me into a working relationship with a wide variety of other professionals: accountants, lawyers, marketing directors, personnel managers, aspiring actors, interior decorators, engineers and entrepreneurs.

Sample issues of Toastmasters' magazine are on the resource table along with a copy of all the articles in my Presentation Skills bibliography.

Who can pronounce the first word on the next tab, "Andragogy in Action?" How many of you have even heard the word before? Andragogy is a big word that means adult education. It rhymes with pedagogy. Andragogy is to training what pedagogy is to teaching.

I was able to obtain copyright permission from Malcolm Knowles, the grandfather of adult education theory, to reproduce a chapter from one of his books that describes adult education basics. Everyone should be familiar with these principles, as they are the foundation of the training model of learning.

The material behind the "Trainer/Trainee Readiness Grid" tab deals with the psychology of getting started. The readiness grid is a tool to help you decide how ready you are and which factors may determine the readiness of your audience. If you are a novice, remember to start small and gradually build your readiness and comfort quotient. Try a joint venture, which will be covered in a later module, if you are feeling uncertain.

We talked about the material behind the seating arrangements tab earlier. Remember that arrangements which have a participatory feel involve your audience more easily.

Audiovisuals appropriately used are powerful tools. Poorly used, they can be a distraction and may actually prevent learning. The material in the handout behind the "Audio Visual" tab covers each type of audiovisual, noting possible pitfalls and best uses for each. When you use visuals you always have to be prepared for mechanical failure. You may have to do the presentation using an alternative method.

The "Handout Architecture" material highlights how to effectively structure printed materials. This is something that Ann Bateson mentioned also. If you are going to teach cite checking, the temptation is to get a Shepard's ™ citator, make a photocopy of a page and use that as a visual, even though it looks like what it is — a quick and dirty copy.

There is a very good example of how copy can be metamorphosized in this section of the handout. A piece of text properly headed and indented, with appropriate white space, a little decoration, a box around the main message is transformed into a piece that catches your eye. The order and organization of the massaged handout are much more memorable to the viewer than the original, unstructured text. It is the difference between a caterpillar and a butterfly.

Ethan Katsh talked about how we have gotten so used to getting information from the printed page that we actually psychologically structure information by how it comes to us off the page. If you are going to use handouts, it will make a difference how the information is :

chunked (structured into visual fields),
queued (ordered spatially),
abstracted (built into a visual system),
filtered (unnecessary information removed) and
cognitive modes mixed (combining strings of text, illustrations, photos, data and diagrams).

The next to the last tab, "Presentation Checklist," is a security blanket. If you put together a presentation quickly, the checklist can be a last–minute review of everything that is important. You may want to make your own list for you and your staff to reference.

The question was asked before the break, should we call the presentation a lecture? In my opinion, certain words, like "lecture," "teaching" and "class" should be avoided in describing presentations, as they suggest school and your audience feels they are finished with formal education. Try to think of words and phrases that are trendy, catch attention, describe the activity or provoke thought. I did a really good orientation session once called "Is There Life After LEXIS?" It dealt with both print and on–line sources and drew attention to the fact that there were still good sources of information in books.

If you look at the fourth item in the Checklist, Under Topic 1, "What," you will see some other ideas. I like "library lambada" because it sounds interactive, sexy, fun and current. What you title the presentation is an essential part of the training framework. To illustrate a program titled, "Learn How to Be a Greek God or Goddess" is training oriented, likely to catch interest and immediate applications imagined, while a class on Greek mythology is pedagogical will probably be of less interest and utility to most people.

Item 3, "When" is extremely important in your planning — not only the time of day but the time of month and the day of the week. I learned from talking to a comedian/taxi driver that on certain days of the week people are in a more jovial and receptive mood than other days. When you are planning, don't just look at your calendar. Investigate other people's calendars and then consider the energy levels on certain days.

The last part of the handout is a reproduction of the quotes on the posters. Most of these quotations come from one of my favorite books, *Information Anxiety*. How many of you have read the book? Is that all? You all must get this book. It is listed in the bibliography and has been a best seller for sometime. I have a "centering" experience every time I open it up.

The book confirms what Ethan was talking about last night. It is a non–linear book. Most books are designed for the reader to start at the beginning and read in one direction to the end. I almost never read books that way. This book is designed to be opened up anywhere — like a database. A large part of the information is written in the margins and consists of succinct one–liners. Actually a good deal of learning is non–linear and is acquired by individuals in a non–logical sequence as their needs and perceptions change.

There are two quotes I especially like and which suggest an over–arching theme to designing training programs.

> "People have a tendency to get hooked on functional fixedness."

Sometimes I think that we as librarians get into functional fixedness modes. We tend to think of books and databases in bibliographic terms instead of as steps in a process. The movie, *The Dead Poet's Society,* shows you how to break out of functional fixedness. Stand on a table and get a new perspective.

The other quote is from Winston Churchill.

> "I always enjoy learning but I don't always enjoy being taught."

The second part of Churchill's message suggests that teachers often do not give students enough control over their learning situations. It also suggests that while learning a new skill people often experience feelings of ineptness and frustration. There are parts of learning that are not a complete joy. This is summed up in another poster quote.

> "In the early stages of acquiring any really new skill, a person must adopt at least a partly anti–pleasure attitude. Who says 'Good,

this is a chance to experience awkwardness and to discover new kinds of mistakes' "?

Ann Bateson is a lecturer who audiences want to hear again and again. She teaches legal research and has a reputation as a top-notch instructor on how to teach legal research. Ann received her MLS and JD from the University of Minnesota and is currently the Assistant Director & Head of Public Services, William Mitchell College of Law Library in St. Paul.

Ann will brief us on how to lecture effectively.

Ann Bateson

One of the first rules of good lecturing is if you promise to do it, you do show up. I promised to be here, so I am, ready to enjoy this opportunity with you. As Marie said, I am very used to lecturing; I'm very comfortable teaching. I like doing both a lot. So feel free to make this a very interactive session, to interrupt whenever you want, and we'll see what we can learn together to make us effective lecturers.

I have four objectives for today's talk, and I would like to go over those objectives with you, since that's one of the principles of good lecturing. But before I do, a comment on the title of my presentation. The title is officially written as "How to Give an Effective Lecture." Dull, right? Wouldn't you be more interested in what I have to say if my presentation had been called, "How to Make Them Want to Listen to You?" If you are going to lecture to others, think about how to describe your topic to them with a title that will hook them. That is my first helpful hint.

Now I would like to do for you today is give you an overview of four concepts about how to use the lecture method effectively when dealing with your young associates or the other people whom you instruct in a law firm setting.

First of all, I would like you to have some concept of when you should use the lecture method. It is not always an appropriate method, and you should know when it is appropriate and when it is not appropriate. Secondly, I'd like to give you some concept of how to go about preparing an effective lecture. However, preparing an effective lecture is only part of the task. So the third set of concepts that I would like for you to take away today are some concepts about how you go about delivering an effective lecture. And finally, I'd like to give you some tools so that you can assess the job that you actually did after you did it.

So again, my four objectives are to teach you: when to use the lecture; how to prepare an effective lecture; how to deliver an effective lecture; and how to assess your own job performance. Now having said that, let me give you a confession. As an academic law librarian, it took me a while to understand that law firm librarians are in the business of teaching as much as academic librarians are. I'll be very honest with you. Last year I taught at AALL's Sacramento Institute on teaching legal research effectively, and I was very surprised to find that probably half of the group that attended that institute were law firm librarians. I was impressed and encouraged by their desire to learn how to teach effectively, and I'm impressed and encouraged by your desire to learn how to do so. It is not an easy task, but let's begin.

Let me tell you what you are up against when you lecture. One researcher said it very well when he reported (and I'll read from the report) that, "in a lecture given by a brilliant scholar with an outstanding topic and a highly competent audience, 10% of the audience displayed signs of inattention within 15 minutes. After 18 minutes a third of the audience and 10% of the platform guests were fidgeting. At 35 minutes everyone was inattentive. At 45 minutes trance was more noticeable than fidgeting; and 47 minutes some were asleep and at least one was reading. A casual check of the audience 24 hours later revealed that most of them recalled only insignificant details, and they were generally wrong." In other words, even when you are top notch, and even when you do it well, it's a darn hard job.

Interestingly enough, another researcher found that typically 31% of the time the people that you are talking to are thinking thoughts entirely unrelated to what you are saying. If I asked you now what were you thinking just a minute ago, it would be interesting to know how many of you were really thinking about effective lecturing. Something else may interest you. As many as 20% of all adults actually very, very much fear getting up and talking to people in any kind of formal setting whatsoever. If you are among that group, don't feel bad about it; you are certainly not alone. There are techniques for overcoming the problem, and that's what we are here to talk about today. So, effective lecturing is darn hard. Now let's learn how to do it.

The first question is: When should you even think about lecturing? And when I say lecturing, especially when I am talking to those of you who are teaching in a law firm environment, lecturing doesn't just mean standing up behind a microphone like this and talking to a large group. It also includes talking to people less formally and talking to small groups. But even if you are using lecturing in the formal sense, there are times when, according to the research, it is more appropriate to use lecturing and times when it's less appropriate. The basic factor that should influence whether you should lecture is the nature of your educational objective. What are you trying to do? Lecturing is appropriate when you are trying to convey information. It's not as appropriate for most other higher–order tasks. And furthermore, even if it's appropriate when you are trying to convey information, it is certainly not always the most effective means to convey information. For example, you all know you can read faster than you can listen to somebody talk, and when you are reading you have the option of going back and reading what you missed. Nevertheless, lecturing can be effective for communicating information.

When should you use lecturing to communicate information? First of all, it's very effective if the information you want to impart isn't really available anyplace else. What kind of information might not be available anyplace else? Perhaps information on the newest research tools in your library. Those tools may not yet be described in any of the standard bibliographic sources.

Lecturing can also be very effective if you want to impart information in a way that makes the presentation unique to a particular group of people. For example, if you have a group of new summer associates and you want to teach that group about how to use the tools in your library, there may not be the written guides that can communicate that information in the same way you can put that information together for that group of associates.

Lecturing is also useful if you want to provide an introduction or an overview to a topic. In a law firm environment, you might want to give an introductory program to your new summer associates on what your law firm considers effective use of both manual and online sources.

Lecturing can also be very appropriate to supplement textual materials, to present different viewpoints, and to help stimulate your listeners' interest in a particular topic. One of the times that lecturing is particularly useful is when you as a lecturer have a new twist on a topic or are able to arrange materials for your listener in a way that nobody else has arranged them.

When is lecturing not so good or not an appropriate technique? It's not really appropriate for developing application skills. You are going to have to design some problems sets or discussion techniques for that.

Lecturing is not as useful to help change attitudes as some other teaching techniques can be.

Lecturing is not particularly effective if your goal is long–term retention. It's not even particularly effective for short–term retention, but it's particularly ineffective for long–term retention.

Lecturing is typically not useful if you've got complex, detailed information (although it can be useful for clarifying complex material).

It's certainly not effective when you have an educational goal where participation is required to accomplish the goal. For example, you probably can't teach people how to lecture effectively if you don't make them do some lecturing along the way.

It is not as effective if your goals are analysis and synthesis as if your goal is information transmission.

So to resummarize this section, the most important question to consider when you think about the presentation style you are going to use in a law firm environment or any environment is: What is your educational objective? Then ask: Is a lecture method an appropriate method to accomplish that educational objective?

If you are going to lecture, it is useful to know what listeners think constitutes an effective lecture. The research studies that I have read say that if you do surveys of listeners, what they tend to say is these are the six most important qualities of a lecturer. (I'll give them to you in the order of one of the last research reports that I read.) First, lecturer should know the topic very very well and explain it understandably. There is no substitute for knowledge; you can't fool listeners. Second, be well organized. Again, you can't fool listeners. If your presentation is not organized, the lack of organization will show immediately, Third, you have to be able to capture attention and hold it. Fourth, it is useful to have interesting material and some material is innately more interesting than other material, but you can make most material interesting. Fifth, your listeners have to think you are competent. Sixth in some studies (although it is first ranked in others) is enthusiasm. You can go a long way if your users really believe that you believe in your subject and that you want desperately for them to understand what you have to teach them. So those are things users think are most important.

Now before we get to the how you do it, I think it's important for you to understand what may be some of your own anxieties about lecturing and about why you may have to do it, so that if you recognize any of these patterns in yourself you can try to overcome them.

There are a couple of possible different reactions to the thought of lecturing. One is severe anxiety or moderate anxiety, and that anxiety can be handled in a couple of different ways. You can erect some defense mechanisms, or you can decide to recognize the anxiety and try to cope with it. If you find yourself exhibiting any of the defense mechanisms, think about how you want to react to them. One author identifies about six defense mechanisms. A typical way some people react to the fear of lecturing or teaching is by denial. They almost deny the fact that they have to do the task; or when they are actually doing the task, they try to deny the reality of what they are doing. One form of denial for a lecturer, for example, would be not looking at the audience. It's the: "Well, I'm here, but I'd rather not be" kind of reaction. Test yourself sometime, or have others observe you. Ask: Do I, if I am standing in front of a group, look like I really want to be there — look like I enjoy being there? So denial is one defense mechanism to the actual hard task of lecturing.

Another one is projection. This is an interesting one. It is basically attributing to your audience some characteristics of yourself. It's saying: They are not prepared, and that's why they didn't learn anything — meaning, I probably wasn't prepared, and that's why they didn't learn anything.

Another characteristic that can indicate some kind of anxiety about lecturing is rationalization. It's using something like: Oh, they are just new associates; they are not worth my time, as a way of saying I don't have to give it a whole lot of attention and energy. Catch yourself if you are giving yourself excuses for not investing the time and energy it takes.

Another defense mechanism — and I love this one because it is mine — is called intellectualization. It's basically spending so much time researching and thinking about your topic that you don't invest the energy it takes to organize it well so you can present it well. Ask yourself: Am I somebody who reads so much that I don't get to the organization and to the rest of the task at hand? Do I get my notes off to the organizer of the program? Am I prepared well in advance, or am I prepared and working on my talk at the last minute?

Another common defense mechanism is substitution, which is doing another activity instead of the proper activity. In the context of giving a lecture, it might mean walking around the room because you don't have something to say. It might mean shuffling papers; it might mean asking questions to fill time, rather than because you have a particular objective in asking those questions.

Finally, another response is just pure repression, actually denying or forgetting that you have a task to do. I know a professor who forgot to show up for a lecture recently. Understanding why and how you may not be prepared as you might like to be can help you overcome your hurdles.

Now that you recognize some of the problems that might exist in yourself in actually getting prepared (or giving a lecture), it's time to turn to the topic of how to prepare an effective lecture. An effective lecture involves two different steps: effective planning and effective presentation. Let's look first at effective planning. If you want to prepare an effective lecture, one of your first tasks is going to be to determine the objectives of your lecture. Your presentation can be no better than what you plan to accomplish. It's critically important that you actually list your objectives for yourself before you go into any classroom presentation, before you go into any law firm presentation. If you can't list them for yourself, you probably don't know what they are, and that is not a very healthy position to be in. So take very seriously the task of defining your objectives.

The second step is to pick the content that you want to cover. The major problem in picking content is that most people try to do too much. Your task is never to teach everything there is to know about your subject to the group you are teaching. Your task is to pick from the mass of material exactly what it is that is most important to get across.

How do you go about picking from the mass of material available to you what might be most important to teach? I have some hints for you. Look at the self–evaluation guides that I hope will be very useful for you to take with you. If you want to get very, very good at doing something, it helps to use checklists of the proper elements of doing that task.

There are a number of checklists or rating guides that are available. These are taken from a book by Nancy Diamond, called *Improv-*

ing Your Lecturing. These checklists are some of the best that I have found. They are quite comprehensive.

The first rating guide, "Content Importance and Suitability," can help you select content. How do you know what is important for you to present? Point one suggests you consider: Is the material that you are interested in material that would be generally accepted by your colleagues as worth knowing? How do you know that? One way you can know is to ask them. Another way to know is to look in some written sources. What do the standard written sources generally say about the topic? Another very logical question to ask in picking content and judging its importance and suitability is: Is this content important for this group of people? One criteria for assessing whether it is important for this group of people is to ask: Is there some immediate applicability to this clientele if I try to teach this topic now? If there is no immediate applicability, perhaps the topic is important but you may want to teach it at a different time.

I won't go over all of the criteria, but importance and suitability and interest to the group are two very important criteria for deciding if the content that you are picking is appropriate for the group that you want to teach that content to.

Another major point that you should remember when picking content is, as I said, don't pick too much. What constitutes too much? If you have a lecture period or an instructional period of 50 minutes, three to five main ideas are the most you can cover. Any more than three to five main ideas and you have lost that group already. An important principle to remember is speeding up how fast you talk does not necessarily speed up how much content your group can learn in a given period of time.

Now when I say three to five main ideas, that doesn't mean you can't give examples, and it doesn't mean you can't give details related to those main ideas. But if you are trying to cover more than three to five main ideas, you are probably covering too much.

Once you pick your content, you must decide how to structure your lecture effectively. You've probably already heard that a good presentation has a good beginning, a good body, and a good ending. What do all of those things mean?

How do you begin a lecture effectively? There are a couple of techniques you can use. First, everybody probably already knows that you try to grab people's attention immediately. People start assessing you from the moment you walk up to a lectern, from the moment you sit down at a seminar table or in a circle, or from the moment you begin whichever teaching technique you use. In fact, people are assessing you from the moment you walk into a room. They are deciding whether you are competent or incompetent, whether you are friendly or unfriendly, and whether they want to be with you or not. So it's very, very important to begin things well.

What are some good techniques for beginning a lecture? Consider these suggestions. You can raise a question that you hope to answer by the end of your teaching period. The question can be as simple as: What does the senior partner at this firm look for in evaluating your research?

Another way to hook your audience with your introduction is to show them the relationship between what you are teaching them and a task they might have expected to perform. What I mean is something like this. Our law firm has just agreed to represent a client in a case that involves a major effort in researching legislative history. In fact, it's quite clear that the case is going to turn on an interpretation of legislative history. One of you in this group will be the law clerk assigned to work on the research, so today we are going to talk to you about how to do effective legislative history research. They know one of them may be assigned the topic, and they are going to be highly motivated to want to learn the material.

A third technique is to relate the lecture or the talk that you are giving that day to content previously covered or to content that will be covered in the future. In other words, put things in context right away so your group knows what you are doing and why you are doing it.

Those are just three possible ways of thinking about how to introduce a lecture. No matter how you introduce it, always give your group an overview of where you are going — the kind of thing that I did today. I said we were going to cover four points: when do you lecture, how do you prepare an effective lecture, how do you deliver an effective lecture, and how do you assess your skills. Give your group that kind of overview. They will have some idea of how long they are going to be there; they will have some idea of the direction in which you are heading. Also, at the beginning of your lecture, if you are discussing a highly technical subject or an unfamiliar subject and the group that you are talking to is unlikely to understand some of the terminology you are using, define your terms. Don't make assumptions about what the group is likely to understand.

How do you go about preparing the body of a lecture effectively? The first point is to remember that your lecture is a set of main points, basically a set of very few main points — three to five if you have a 50–minute time period — with associated examples, illustrations, exceptions and so on — but it is basically a set of three to five main points that you arrange in some kind of logical order. It is important for you to think of what might constitute a logical order. Let me give you some examples of logical orders. Some are appropriate for some lecture topics; others are appropriate for different lecture topics.

Cause and effect might be an appropriate way to arrange the main points of your discussion.

Another method is to use a time–sequence principle. If you are teaching your clientele about how to do legislative history research and what kinds materials are important in that process, the materials easily lend themselves to a time sequence. The bill is introduced, it goes to committees, it goes to the floors of the houses, it goes to conference committees, so the materials themselves develop in a time sequence. Similarly, if you are teaching your new associates about administrative law materials in your library, you may want to begin with the development of administrative agencies. Historically, without the development of administrative agencies, there would be no administrative law materials. Without knowing why agencies developed, for what purposes they developed, and how they go about generating materials, there would be no materials that your students needed to know about.

It is also possible to use a problem/solution approach. This is the research problem that we have. Let's brainstorm about proper research strategies. There is no one and only solution. There are many solutions, and it is appropriate to start with the problem, and then to have a discussion about what solutions might be. That's one very good organizational principle.

Another organizational principle would be a compare–and–contrast principle. With Westlaw and LEXIS, we do it all of the time. How are these systems alike, how are they different, what do you want to know about similarities and differences?

Another organizational principle is to teach by going from examples to a rule. You can have a number of examples and see if your students can derive the rule or rules from the examples that you use.

Those are just some of the organizational principles that are available to you. Whichever you choose, your students, your listeners, should be able to grasp the principle that you have chosen.

Once you have picked your key points and chosen your organizational principle and put your key points in order, then it's very, very useful to develop lots of examples and illustrations for the points you are using. You never know which of those points may be very easy for your students to understand and which may be very hard for them to understand, so it's useful to have lots of examples and illustrations handy. They help make presentations more interesting and you can use them if you need them, and you can drop them if you are running short on time or if you don't seem to need them for the group you have. Examples and illustrations build in flexibility.

It is really important when you are lecturing to build in some time flexibility. You will usually have more material than you have time to present. I can almost always guarantee it. When you write materials, when you outline, you are working on paper. When you are actually up in front of a group, if you are doing it well, you are looking at people, you are waiting for responses, you are trying to judge if they are with you, and you are giving them time to ask questions. So, you usually won't get through as much as you think you will. Therefore, it is always useful to know which of the material you have is your throw–away material. If you run out of time, if you don't have time to cover the material, know what material you can drop if you want to or what material you can most easily carry over to the next time that you meet with the group.

In addition to preparing examples and building in flexibility, you should plan for transitions between the three to five main points that you have selected. Your listeners should be able to say, for example, OK, we have talked about when to use the lecture, we've talked about how to prepare it. They should be able to feel, next what we are going to talk about is how to deliver it. The transitions should be clear. They should be specific, and they should be obvious to your listeners.

It is really important not only that you pick your content well, know your objectives and structure your presentation well. You should also be able to end your presentation well. There is nothing worse than leaving your audience hanging and wondering if you have accomplished what you wanted to. There is nothing worse than closing your books, packing up your materials and saying, "That's all," because it's lunch time or that's all the time you have today. Your audience deserves the security of knowing you've done what you set out to do. So how do you provide closure to a lecture effectively? Well, you can briefly summarize what you did. You can provide the summary yourself, or sometimes a more effective technique actually is ask your students to summarize. You can, for example, ask your students how they expect to use the material that you have just presented for the day. There are many different summarizing techniques. Or rather than summarize, you can relate the material that you have just covered to what you covered the previous day or to what you might be covering at a future day.

As you prepare your lecture, you should plan for a variety of activity during the lecture. Recall that most people can only listen to lecture content for about 15 minutes and, as my researchers' examples showed, their attention starts dropping off, and they start to think about other things. So one of the most important principles of being an effective teacher is, yes, use the lecture, but consider using it for 15 to 20 minutes stretches; then vary activities. Let me give you an example of an activity you could use in a lecture like this one — when you get to the topic of Organizing Content. On the last page of your handout are two lists. The first is a random list of letters. You can fold that page in two and have people look at the first half of this list for one minute. After that one minute, have them write down how many of those random order letters they can recall. Then have them look at the bottom list. It has some groupings that contain strange words which may not mean a lot to them individually. Have them look at that list for X number of minutes and ask them how many of the words they recall. This kind of exercise is appropriate to this kind of topic. It quickly reinforces the idea that a principle of organization assists memory.

For almost any topic on which you are teaching, there are break-up exercises you can use, and I strongly encourage you to use some. One way to vary activities is to have people form pairs for a one- or two-minute session and respond to questions like: What one question do you have about the topic that hasn't been answered yet? What one additional point would you like the speaker to cover? What one concept that has been presented doesn't seem very clear to you and would you like some further explanation of? So there are many ways in which you can break up a lecture. Please consider doing so.

Once you have prepared an effective lecture, that's only part of the battle. The next part of the battle is the delivery. Delivery is critically important, although don't fool yourself. No matter how good you are, good delivery can't substitute for lack of preparation and lack of knowledge. On the other hand, all the preparation and all of the knowledge in the world can fall very flat. So it really is important to think about the kinds of delivery skills that you want to use.

You may want to consider using audiovisuals for your presentation. Generally a very important principle is to do so. Now I'm a little bit insecure whenever I go to new places, and one of the principles of using audiovisuals is to make sure you have a setup where things will work, so I did handouts today instead of overheads. There are some materials that are better in handout form than in overhead form. One of the things that law librarians typically do too often is they photocopy pages of books, put them on overheads, and think that people will be able to see and interpret what they have done. Not so.

Another very poor technique in using audiovisuals is to become loaded down with audiovisuals. You never have time to use as many as you think you do, and if you are going to use them at all, give your audience time to see them. Give them time to see them and use them, or else give them to your audience in a form that they can take home and think about later. There is nothing worse than the Whip–Em–By Syndrome on an overhead projector. If you have 20 audiovisuals and a 50 minute class, you have too many audiovisuals. It takes time to put each one on the machine and take it off and say a word about it. Think about time when you think about audiovisuals.

There are other issues related to audiovisuals. You have to think about availability of equipment. If you are in a law firm you are probably competing for any equipment you might want to use with others in your department, so availability and scheduling may be a problem. Troubleshooting can be a problem. If you are going to use any piece of equipment, make sure you set it up beforehand. Make sure you test it beforehand. Go to your room beforehand. Actually running through your AV material is incredibly important. Don't use somebody's stuff, don't show a film, without actually having previewed it first.

Other important principles. Keep your AV material or your handouts around long enough to keep interest high, but not so long that they totally distract attention or that they become old and boring. If you are using AV materials of any kind, whether it's handouts or overheads, reveal your content gradually, one point at a time. Tell students when you want them to be looking at the materials. Develop some guidelines for using them. Make sure you have time for some applications. Also, be sure that any audiovisual you use, either prepared material or your own writing on the board, is legible and very readable for the size of the room that you have and the kind of material that you are using. So that part of delivery, audiovisual delivery, if you are going to use those techniques, is incredibly important.

In addition to using proper audiovisual techniques, there are vocal techniques that are important. In your handouts, and again I won't go over all of the points with you, after the content handouts, which covered importance and suitability, followed by organization, the next set of handouts breaks down presentation skills. In the first one are some of the style skills — voice characteristics, for example, and nonverbal communication techniques. It's very apparent when I say it, but you may not think about it when you speak: Can your voice be easily heard? Test it. You can ask somebody in the back of a room if you are in a big room to raise their hand if they can hear you. Check also: Is your pitch right? Is your volume right? Is your speed right? Ask your listeners sometime. If you don't ask them in the middle of the class, you can ask them at the end of a class. Did I talk at about the right speed for you? Did I mumble too much? Was I clear? Voice characteristics can be incredibly important. If you can willingly ask people to observe you now and then and to give you all the feedback they can, that's a marvelous technique. It is very, very hard to overcome the fear of having people observe you. But if you can take the initiative and ask people to observe you, you will get the kind of feedback that you need to make some of your verbal techniques much better. Somebody else can tell you much easier than you will pick up on your own, for example, if you have any of those voice mannerisms such as um or ah that annoy listeners so much.

An observer can also identify for you some of your nonverbal communication patterns that may affect the quality of your presentation. All of us have different mannerisms. Some of them are very distracting in a teaching situation; some of them are very effective and quality–enhancing in a teaching situation. Let me give you an easy example. Some mannerisms are socially acceptable, some are not. Rubbing your cheek like this as you are trying to think through an issue might be socially acceptable. Picking your nose or scratching your crotch, law students do notice. You get these kinds of things written down in student evaluations. It is useful for you to know — do I have any irritating mannerisms? Do I have any effective mannerisms that I want to keep? Take a look at the list of presentation style characteristics. Both verbal and nonverbal communication techniques can be incredibly important to you.

In addition to considering your own verbal and nonverbal communication techniques, it is important to consider the physical environment that you are lecturing in. If you are going to use a room as a teaching room, it's very important to check things like the temperature of the room. It is important to check to see if there is construction going on outside the room. If so, you might not want to use the room on a particular day. So take a look at the physical characteristics of your room. Take a look at room layout. Some layouts are much more conducive to promoting interaction than other layouts. Take a look at sight lines and audiovisual capacity. If you are ever speaking, go into the room before you actually use it to be sure it is the kind of room that you need.

After you give a lecture, how do you start assessing your lecture skills? How do you figure out if you've done a good job?

One of the first things that I would suggest to you is do a little post-lecture review. Stop somebody and say: Can I talk to you a minute? What do you think about what happened today? What did I do well? What could I have done better? People will be very glad to stop after a class and talk to you. Another way you can assess how well you are doing is to look at the behavior of people during your presentation. Are their heads dropping? Are they reading newspapers? Are they wandering off? Their behavior is a very good clue to you. You can also create some formal evaluations, and you can do them for one program or you can do them for a series of programs. In academic environments, we all get teacher evaluations at the end of every semester. I would suggest that whether you are in an academic environment or an instructor in a law firm environment, don't wait that long. You don't want to wait until after you've done a whole series of programs to find out if you have some major improvement to make. Prepare a little checklist. You can have a little checklist that takes the student at the end of a class, or end of a law firm presentation, one minute to fill out.

Consider audiotaping and videotaping yourself. You are doing some of that here. It's a very painful process, and I will admit I have not done it. I do it for everybody else all of the time, and I'm one of those people who most hates to have it done. But I have a lot of people come and observe me, and that's a very useful technique. Actually watching yourself is painful, but it is well worth doing. Colleague review is also an exceptionally useful method. Again, if you can get over the fear of having somebody watch you, if you can take the initiative, if you can be the first one to say to somebody, please come and help me, I'd like your input, you've come a very long way to being effective.

There is one other point I want to make. I once read a marvelous quotation. It went something like this. You spend a lot of time collecting information. Don't just shoot it out there like a gun. What you really want to do is send it out there like a boomerang, so that it will come back to you, and so that the students whom you hoped to learn something catch it and pitch it back to you, and the cycle continues and the progress goes on.

I wish you success in all your lecturing. Can I answer any questions for anyone?

Q: [Inaudible]

A: You are absolutely right. You have to be able to read the audience you have and in some situations an audience reaction may mean one thing, and in a different situation an audience reaction may mean something else. The way you can get at the meaning of a particular audience in behavioral response is to do a little spot check. Ask the person who is doing something that indicates distraction a question based on what you said. The response is a good clue to their level of attentiveness.

I used to work at the telephone company when I was a high school student, and they taught the principle of overlapping. You were supposed to be doing two things at once. When you were pulling the cord out of the switch control board with one hand, you were supposed to be dialing a telephone number with the other. Law school students who are pressured for time typically do try to do two or three things at a time. It may not be an insult to you, and they may be learning. You're right.

Q: [Inaudible]

A: Absolutely. Don't make somebody sit for two–hour stretches. We do that at faculty meetings at our place, but the faculty are sophisticated enough so everybody knows that you get up and get your coffee when you want, and you go to the bathroom when you want. People forget to tell people that it's OK to do that, or they forget to structure in the breaks so that people can do that. There's the old saying that the mind can only absorb what the seat can endure, that kind of thing. It's really true. Don't expect the impossible of your listeners. Make it fun for them. Make them want to be there.

Q: [Inaudible]

A: There are definitely learning differences in people. For example, some people like to learn orally, and some people prefer to learn by reading. One of the ways that you deal with learning differences is to try to provide a variety of opportunities and methods of learning. For instance, it's useful to have backup handouts or backup readings on reserve that cover your lecture material or similar material in a different way.

Your objective in doing a lecture may be to pick out and emphasize some of the complex material that students might have a harder time learning on their own, but it's useful to use some backup methods. A backup can be to videotape the lecture that you are doing so those who learn best by watching and listening twice have the opportunity to do so. Definitely create as many backup opportunities as you can.

When you talk about different learning techniques, I might add some very interesting research on the best method for taking notes and whether teachers should teach students how to take notes. One study says that the average student takes about 11% of the proper notes he or she should. The good students maybe take about 55% of the correct notes. Students take a lot of incorrect notes. It's pretty well established that students will write down anything the teacher puts on the board, so if you think what you have to say should be something that the student copies down, put it on an overhead, put it on the board.

There have been studies done that ask: Do you give students a total outline of your presentation? Do you give them a partial outline? How do you do it? Most of the research in that area seems to say, give the students a partial outline. If you give them the whole outline, they stop listening.

One of the ways in which students learn is by translating what you are saying into their own kind of note–taking form. So definitely there are differences of opinion on how to do a lot of these things. There is not difference of opinion on the fact that students do learn differently, so you need to consider a variety of techniques, and the differences are the best argument for not lecturing all of the time. It is not the preferred learning method for a lot of students.

Q: [Inaudible]

A: You can handle those handouts any way you want, and you should in many cases hold them hostage until you get to the point at which you want to use them. You can pass out the materials at the end of the class, and as I said in the material about overheads, if when you are presenting material and you are on point 1 on your overhead, a standard good teaching technique is to cover points 2, 3, and 4 so that your students aren't getting way ahead of you and therefore not listening to the material you are currently trying to get them to understand.

[Due to audio difficulties, the remainder of Ann Bateson's answer is unavailable.]

Marie Wallace

In much of the law library literature, we read that most of the students and new associates arrive at firms ill prepared, ignorant, green and lacking in research skills. I don't think that is entirely true. It has been my experience that a fair number of them are quite sophisticated and prepared to ask good questions. They may have clerked for a judge, spent a summer at a large firm with an excellent library staff or be a natural researcher. When you prepare your training programs you have to consider people with relatively advanced skills.

Let me give you my own experience. Suppose you have a summer associate who is the producer of the *Commander Legal Research* videos. Further suppose that same student is going to be a new associate in your firm. What do you do? In my case, I thought the best thing is to invite him to speak at the conference. He is a member of our target audience, on the one hand. On the other hand, he is involved in the same endeavor that we are — trying to teach research and create presentations that are relevant, instructive and entertaining.

Out next speaker is David Feldman. Some of you have met Dave where he manned the Legal Star Communications exhibit booth at AALL in Reno for Bob Berring's Commando videotapes. Let me give you a bit of background on Dave. As I mentioned, he produced the Commando videotapes and is a third–year student at Boalt Law School in Berkeley. He grew up in L.A. and was a TV news producer before he went to law school. In law school he joined forces with Bob to create the Commando tapes. Dave is going to describe the long, winding road from student to research video producer to new associate.

Bridging the Gap – Law School to Law Firm

David Feldman

Thank you very much. It is a pleasure to be here. I want to thank Marie especially for giving me another opportunity to miss classes. I feel a bit nervous coming up here and speaking to you. We were just watching some of those presentation tapes, and I was taking careful note of people shuffling and touching themselves and I'm glad I have this huge podium to hide behind. But in a sense it is kind of nerve-racking. I feel as though I am interviewing for a job in some way with 40 firms at the same time. In any case I do appreciate the invitation. It is a unique opportunity for someone in my position to be here and it's funny because Marie calls my talk (I don't want to call it a lecture), "Bridging the Gap." That's an interesting title. I suppose it lends itself to two questions.

One is what is the gap, and the other is what is the bridge? In turn I think the gap is what someone like myself learns as a law student in terms of legal research, or doesn't learn. And how he takes that with him into the law firm experience. The other side of the gap is the actual legal research training a law student should have, either coming in as a clerk or operating as a young associate. There is a wide distance between the two, as I found out quickly during my first year of clerking.

The second question is what is the bridge? Well, I guess that's me, which is hard to define. I think part of that comes from my background. As Marie mentioned I was a television news producer for five years before I went to law school, between the time of undergraduate and graduate school. Then I also have the experience of learning legal research in the law school environment, and I really divide that into two categories that I call pre "Bob" and post "Bob."

The third is my work outside of law school as a contributor to and creator of the Commando Legal Research Video Tape Series, which reemphasized all of the things I didn't know in legal research and helped me focus in on them. What I'd like to do is briefly talk about those three different areas. I don't know if that's going to be instructive in any definitive sense, but it may help lend some perspectives to where I come from sitting somewhat on both sides of the fence as a law student who receives information, and also contributing as a vendor who provides information.

My background coming out of school was a business degree, and I really didn't want to go to work for a business. So, what do you do? Well, in my case I went traveling. I wondered around the country for about six months until I ran out of money and then I came home. I came back to Los Angeles and tried to figure out what am I going to do now? The answer I came up with was that I knew I enjoyed photography. I had done some photography working for student newspapers as an undergrad, so I picked up my 35mm camera and I became a freelance photographer. I shot things like weddings, bar mitzvas, headshots and a lot of public relations events. It was during one of those public relations events that I made the leap into television news, or attempted to.

I was shooting for the National Cable Television Association, and the featured keynote speaker at this convention was Ted Turner. Prior to Ted's making his keynote speech in front of the entire convention, he had a press conference. At this press conference there were about 30 members of the press and photographers like myself and some reporters. Ted got up there, "the mouth of the south" as he is known, and he made a fantastic little presentation. Everybody was awestruck and at the end of the presentation he came out into the audience. He walked around and was meeting people and shaking hands and everybody was quite taken with him. My only prior media experience had been as a deejay at Berkeley when I was an undergrad. KALX 90.7 FM in Berkeley.

So I walked up to Ted when the moment seemed right and I said, "Hello Mr. Turner, my name is Dave Feldman. I went to UC Berkeley; I was in college radio."

He said, "College radio, oh yes that's wonderful. We really enjoy radio. You know I've got Headline Radio, Headline News. Radio is wonderful, it's fantastic."

I said, "Well I think you are doing a marvelous service; CNN is a wonderful enterprise; I know it's going to do fantastically well. Twenty–four hour news seems like an idea that is going to catch on and frankly, I would like to work for you." He looked at me, put his hand on my shoulder, and he said, "Sure son, everybody would."

But, he did give me a business card. I guess already then I was starting to employ some of Bob's Commando Techniques because I used the telephone and I called the person on the business card, who was some corporate communications director.

He said, "What do you do?" I said, "I don't know." He said, "Where are you living?" "Los Angeles." He suggested that I talk to a person in California. I called him.

He said, "What can you do?" I said, "I don't know." He said, "We have an intern program. You work for two or three days a week without pay and that's what you do; you are a slave."

I said, "Well I guess that's what I'll do." And that's really how I got my foot in the door in television news. I'd had a little production background but nothing formal. I really learned by doing in the TV news field. I came in as an intern; I learned how to write teases, edit video-tapes, and eventually write news story copy. Three months of doing that went by and they started a new show that was anchored both in Atlanta, Georgia and Los Angeles. I managed to get on as an associate producer of the West Coast segment of that show. I found it very exciting.

At the same time, to cover all of my bases I took the LSAT's, because you never know. But with TV news starting to take off a little bit for me, I went for that. I continued in that until the person who was my supervising producer went off to Omaha, Nebraska to work in local television news there and I moved up a little bit in the ranks at CNN. Then he called me about ten months down the line and said, there's an opening for a producer in Des Moines, Iowa.

After much consideration, I decided to move to Des Moines, Iowa and become the daily 6 P.M. news producer for the NBC affiliate there. Since I didn't know much about Iowa, I relied heavily on my anchors and staff for determining which stories would be important to our viewers. And in one particular humorous incident, I again found myself saved from embarrassment by following Bob's rule about updating and evaluating your information.

In this particular case I noticed on the wire services, both UPI and AP, a story that said "Truck overturned on the highway 8,000 pigs dead." Now, I thought about that and to me that sounded like a lot of bacon. I am visualizing 8,000 pigs strewn across a highway about an hour and one–half from Des Moines, and I am thinking to myself, "My God, this is Iowa style television news."

Now, it is an unfortunate truism of TV news that the visual sometimes dictates the story. If you have a story about arms control and a great video of the domino championships, a lot of times those domino championships are going get on the air ahead of your arms story.

So, I saw this story about 8,000 pigs and it sounded like something we should cover. So, I went to Scott Pope, my "Iowan who knows Iowa." I said, "Scott, look at this story — 8,000 pigs. Am I mistaken or is that not a lot of hog — is that massive pig carnage or what? That could be one–quarter mile of pigs." I started thinking we could scoop this. I started putting things in gear. I was getting ready to call a helicopter to get a camera crew up in the helicopter, pull them out, pull another crew, re–write the lead, do all of this stuff with about an hour left until showtime.

Then it occurred to me that I had better be sure I have this right before I put this whole machinery in gear. Let me call UPI and try to verify things. So I put in a call into UPI. I said "Hi, this is Dave Feldman of WHO and I am seeing your story here about the 8,000 pigs on the highway and I am just wondering if that is correct."

He said, "Oh, Dave, it is a good thing you called. We were just about to run a little correction." I said, "Oh, you mean there wasn't a truck that overturned." He said, "No, the truck overturned, but it wasn't 8,000 pigs, it was 8 sows and pigs."

I was glad I made that call. I could just imagine what would have happened if we had this whole helicopter crew there and this little pick–up truck with a few little pigs on the highway. So, that was part of the experience to learn to check facts and learn to do accurate, updated research.

At the same time, and I will just mention this briefly, my interest in law got piqued again in Iowa. Without going into detail, we were involved in a very interesting first amendment case that eventually worked its way up to the Iowa Supreme Court after I left. Throughout the case I was involved with the lawyers of the station preparing interrogatories, answering depositions and things like that.

I realized for a time that I was almost having a better time working with them, and was starting to be a little more interested intellectually. It dawned on me that maybe I should just cover my bases again, and I started making applications to law schools.

In the meantime while I did that, my TV news career took another jump and I moved to Atlanta, Georgia, where I went back to work for CNN producing international news. Although it was a bigger arena, in some ways it wasn't quite as interesting as Iowa because I was more involved in the local scene in a small news organization than in the network scene, but it was still interesting.

Nevertheless, when acceptances came in and I found myself accepted to Boalt Hall, I had to make a decision. I opted to go to law school. So, that is why I ended up there. The first viable lesson I learned in law school was that as a news producer I had always written copy succinctly — the sky is blue. That to me was succinct. I found out actually that in law school, the sky generally appears to seem to be blue when you are outside during the daytime.

So, I had to reorient myself a little bit. They have a saying or axiom in law school and I guess most of you have heard it — and that is — the first year they scare you, the second year they work you, and the third year they bore you. That is somewhat of a truism, and I definitely fit right into that mold as a first-year law school student.

Even with my background, I was doing study groups and outlining everything and reading every case. It took me an hour to read a case. Somewhere in the background there was this course called legal research. Right off the bat you were hit with the idea that this didn't matter as much. First of all because it wasn't graded; it was pass/fail. Staying to the far end of the efficiency fairness continuum, I just figured I had to put my energies where the grades are and legal research was going to have to be handled on a basis of as much as I needed to learn at that time was what I would learn. The rest would have to wait.

So, my general summation of the first year of legal research was that it was there. That was my exposure to it. I realized how little legal research knowledge I had when I went to clerk as a first-year summer associate. I went to a medium-sized law firm in Los Angeles that had about 60 attorneys. I am not going to mention any names but I doubt anybody is here from the firm.

They didn't have a law librarian and I didn't know it mattered, because that was not one of the things that came up when I was interviewing. My experience as a first-year clerk was, I guess, somewhat typical of how a lot of clerks still come into a lot of firms. I was given certain projects. I was told generally the parameters. I would try to figure out what they really meant and I would go off to this place called a library.

I had so little experience at that time with the materials, even California state materials; I really didn't know the difference between Witkin and CALJUR. I guessed they were similar. They both talked about the law, but I didn't appreciate that one might be a treatise and one might be an annotated code, and there is a difference between state annotated codes and federal annotated codes — things I think are pretty basic now.

But at the time I was just lucky to find the books in the library. I remember the frustrating experience of trying to find definitive answers to real-world legal questions. And I never knew the calculus of trying to figure out when to stop because I never knew if I had been everywhere. That was a big problem, and I think one issue I would flag for new clerks. In keeping with the "Bridging the Gap" theme, there is a huge gap between applying the legal research process to a legal issue and the usual classroom research exercise which is designed to have you find an answer.

Coming into a law firm this is something you get hit with immediately, because if they had the answers they wouldn't ask you to do it. So, I went back to school. And I took what I thought at the time would be a blow-off course, which was Bob Berring's course in advanced legal research.

It turned out there were 200 other people in the class that thought it would be a blow-off course, too. But nobody blew it off. They all went and they went there every day, which was unusual because everybody at this time was looking for classes they could avoid if they weren't interesting.

One of the things that stirred my imagination was sitting in this classroom with 200 other students listening to Bob and actually feeling I was learning something and laughing a lot because, of course, the lectures were hilarious. And watching the other people around me because they were learning and laughing a lot, too.

So, my mind started working. Bob would wheel in these book carts and he would show us these materials and you got a feel but you really couldn't get into them, and it occurred to me that this subject lent itself to the interactive nature of video. So I approached Bob one day with some ideas. We met in his office and we talked about different things and different assignments. And I approached the subject of videotapes, and explained to him some of my background.

I asked him what he thought of this course being put in a video format. Interestingly, it was good timing because he had thought about videos and had done some thinking on the subject, but didn't really have a full conception of how it might work out and what would be involved in putting something together. This was where I was able to lend a little experience. I knew some production people in Los Angeles with a company called Creative Video that had already done a lot of educational and training films in different areas for colleges and industry.

That was really the genesis of the Commando Legal Research tape series. Now that I had taken Bob's course and in the interim had shot the Commando Legal Research videotapes, I felt infinitely more confident going into a law firm as a second–year clerk.

I remember being taken on a tour of the library in the Century City office at O'Melveny and Pat Smith was showing me things. I knew what they were. Yes, that is a looseleaf service and that is a periodical index and there is a copyright treatise and I understand how they all fit together. It was a very good feeling. I had worked with these tools a lot and I had seen them.

I also kept in mind the rules and commandments and the things we had tried to establish in the Commando Legal Research Series, and the first one, of course, is Bob's first rule — "Find someone who has done the work for you." That became my guiding principle while I was a second–year clerk. I hope I am not revealing anything to Marie that I shouldn't reveal, but I would apply this rule that when I got those difficult research assignments at O'Melveny — I'd turn to this very cool tool called the memo book.

The memo book had an index to every prior memo written by associates and summer clerks on a particular subject and it was indexed. So when I was handed a subject and a research problem, I was more focused on asking questions of the assigning attorney because I could say, — "Do you want me to concentrate on secondary sources? Do you want me to concentrate on primary sources? Should I start in the codes? Who do you think are the big heavyweights here? Are we looking for a persuasive authority or are we looking for something on point in terms of the case?"

And by asking more pointed questions, I could get a better idea of what that attorney wanted me to do. Once I had that I would go to the O'Melveny memo book and find everything even close to the subject, incorporate that into my memo, do the research that needed to be done for this specific task and update that research, and turn it in. I turned out a lot more work in my second summer and I felt good about that. I think that was the big difference for me between my second summer and my first summer.

I am not saying that a person has to have a course with Bob Berring or he or she has to have Commando Legal Research. But I think it is true if you don't have something like that in your second year, the clerks coming in are going to be as unprepared as I was as a first–year clerk when you get them. And you probably do.

These overpaid students come into these summer programs and you think, "My God, they don't know anything." Somebody said to me last night that he (or she) became a law librarian because he or she liked working with children. I guess, in a sense, that is what we seem to be when we come in as summer people.

From the summer person's perspective, I think they come in from the perspective of what I call the "three goods" — They want to have good pay, they want to do good work, and they want to have a good time. I think that is the perspective summer people take coming in.

Now, the good pay seems to take care of itself. I think that the good work, if it is done well, puts them at ease and gives them more time to have a good time. So, I think they can all work together.

What I don't think summer people get, and maybe this is something I can share, is they don't know who you (the librarians) are and how much you can help them. They don't know how to go for it. I think they would be a lot more comfortable coming to a law librarian who is very knowledgeable and has all of this expertise rather than go to another associate or a peer or to a partner. I look on law librarians now as the Great Asset because usually the librarian is not going to make or break your offer, but they can be very helpful in your securing that offer. And by nature, I think they are very helpful.

Where I would like to go from here is to talk about how law librarians can impart more to the students at an earlier time. I guess in your own firms you have to deal with the hierarchy and bureaucracy and you are always working with the training people. But, as much as you can emphasize to these people the function and the importance of your early interaction with summer associates, the better it is for both the firm and the students. And, I think summer associates will really appreciate it if they know you are there. It is unfortunate that a lot of them just don't realize what a great resource you are.

Before I conclude, I'd just like to share a couple of quick stories you might enjoy.

In making the Commando Tapes, one of the reasons I learned so much is because we shot the same scenes 10 to 15 times. You may feel uncomfortable looking at these videos of yourself, and think, "Why can't I do it like Bob Berring?" He gets up there and he does those videos and he is funny and he has presence. However even with Bob, as great as he is, it is not a one-shot deal.

It was interesting because I found myself in the awkward position when we were shooting the videos of having to say, "Bob, can you do it one more time with a little emphasis," and thinking, "You know, he hasn't even graded my exam yet." But we made it through. In fact, when we produced the tapes, it took only a week to shoot everything. The post-production on those tapes is what really took the longest time.

Once in a while near the late afternoon, right before we would be going for a take, I would see Bob pulling little things out of his pocket. I was thinking, "Bob, are you taking pills; are you taking vitamins?" Actually, they were chocolate coated coffee beans. It is a helpful tip, if you need that little pick-me-up before that next training. But the point is that when doing any kind of video, you need to be sensitive to your on-camera person's needs whether it be coffee, chocolate, water or whatever.

I don't know if I have added much. I would just like to end on some thoughts for in-house video production in your own firm. I think it is a good idea, because as some people have mentioned, the generation of law students is the video generation. If a law student is 23 years old as a summer clerk today, it means he or she was born in 1967. That means he or she was 14 years old when MTV debuted. This is the MTV generation of law students, and that is a truth we must take into consideration.

I think we have to prepare for that. In general, they are more print-oriented than the average student, but they are still much more inclined toward the visual area. I think the more you can use visuals, in areas of research and training that are appropriate for visuals, the better off it will be and the better off it will be received.

I just want to give you, and I don't mean for you to take notes on this because it is just off the top of my head, what I call the five "P's" of production.

The first "P" is planning. Obviously with any enterprise, especially a videotape presentation, you want to plan it. You want to plan out when you are going to do it. As I mentioned, if you do it when the instructor is tired or has not prepared well himself, then it is not going to be a quality preparation. You want to plan it. You want to plan out how long you think the end result is going to be and you want to plan out the content to a point of having an outline. Some people work well from outlines and others need to have every word written out. Whoever is going to be doing the presentation — you want to focus in on what their strengths are in front of the camera. These exercises, like doing some practice videos, are good as well. And even at this early preparatory stage, keep in mind who is the audience.

The second "P" I would try to stress is Professionalism. Now there are going to be limitations on that. If you are working in the law firm environment, more than likely you are going to work with one–half inch format, which is limiting in terms of the quality of the image. If you have access to three–quarter inch cameras and you can work with them or you can hire a camera operator and your firm can afford to invest the money, you will end up with a higher quality product. It suddenly comes across to people, when they are watching something whether or not it looks as if it were professionally done. To the extent that you can invest in it, I would say do so. If you can't invest in it, at least try to have some professional consultation in terms of putting together your program. Also, graphics and video inserts help keep people more tuned in than a static shot of a talking head.

The third "P" I would mention is Point of View. Now, what I mean by this is that you have to realize who is looking at this. If the student is going to be engaged, you have to take the student's point of view in the presentation. I have taken two cross–country flights this year. One was on Continental and one was the one here on United. On Continental Airline they do these videos of the in–flight preparation. Here is how to do seat belts, here is how your seat cushion floats. On Continental, it was a female stewardess sitting alone in an airplane buckling her seat belt, grabbing the flotation cushion, reaching up for the mask, casually as they kind of drifted down. It was not any more engaging than watching a flight attendant doing it normally. On the United flight, it was interesting because they had the plane passengers themselves. Here are the people coming onto the plane, they are putting stuff in the overhead bins, they are sitting down and as part of the natural course they are buckling their seat belts. It is as if there is a story here because this is a planeload of passengers. When they had the oxygen masks come out, the plane was full of passengers. They came to a halt, the masks ricocheted out and you felt like watching it because this is the point of view that you have as a passenger. So it made a little bit more of an impression, and suddenly it makes a difference in watching something like that. So, I would say keep in mind the point of view of the student when you are making your training videos.

The fourth thing I would mention is what I call Punch. Punch can be anything — humor, a hook, something that grabs. That is why we call Bob's tapes Commando Legal Research. At first it was going to be "How to Do Advanced Legal Research in the Law Firm Environment When You Are Just a Student, etc., etc." It doesn't say anything. As Marie was saying earlier about hanging your hat on something, you need a hook in your title. That is why Commando Legal Research and the Commando Commandments stick in people's heads. So, I recommend that you use humor. If you are going to use some other mechanism, whether it is the fear situation of not having the project done or whatever it is, focus on it, center on it and have that kind of punch.

Finally don't forget the last "P", which I would call Promotion. I think if you are going to create something and you are going to put the time and energy into it, you want to have the follow-up of putting it out there. Use the company newsletters, create posters, put things in people's mailboxes, plan out an activity around the presentation of the video. In some way try to tie it all together and to make it an event or as much of an event as possible. After all, as far as summer people go, I know they come there looking for events. And if you can make your training session into an event, it will be just another reason for them to come.

Options for Teaching Research

OVERVIEW

Gitelle Seer

Our goal in this module is to help you identify and exploit the different resources that are available to you when you are putting together an in-house training program.

In talking to people over the last few days, I know we all agree on a couple of really basic things. The research skills of our users are not what they ought to be. We, as librarians, are certainly one of the key players in our firms in putting a program together. We have the knowledge, we are generally supportive, we are generally nonjudgmental, and as somebody mentioned yesterday, teaching in our firms is one of the few ways that we have to enhance our status. So that is something that we really have to latch on to.

In my firm, we just started a Needs Assessment Program. We brought a consultant in and sent a survey around to all our attorneys to determine what they felt their training needs were, whether they felt they were being met, what training opportunities they were familiar with, what they were taking advantage of.

A lawyer training and development committee was formed and I was asked to be on that committee, and I thought that was very enlightened of my firm. Then I got a copy of the survey to comment on and in the section on identifiable skills, there was nothing at all about research. There were trial advocacy skills and negotiation techniques and legal writing. Nothing at all about research, so of course I added it in, but I think that sort of shows us what a low premium is placed on that and it sort of put me in my place.

I would like to tell you just how this meeting is going to work and introduce the speakers, because I know those are the people you really came to hear. We are going to have each of our five panelists speak for about twenty minutes with a ten minute question–and–answer session after each one. Starting in the reverse order in which they are going to speak, at the very end of the table at my left is Ellen Miller of Harvard,

Karen Brunner from Riker Danzig in Morristown, New Jersey, Stephanie Heacox, Sullivan & Cromwell in New York, Timm Whitney from Morgan, Lewis in New York and Jean O'Grady, Shea & Gould, New York. I think most of you probably know Jean, she is the Director of Legal Information Services at Shea and Gould in New York, and Jean has an in–house training program in place in her firm and is going to talk to you about how to put it all together and get the support and credibility that you need.

Jean O'Grady

You know just picking up on what Gitelle was saying, when I began doing research for this, I reviewed some of the *American Lawyer* articles about summer associate programs and one of the things that horrified me was that one of the ways that the associates rated their program was an inverse proportion to the amount of time that they had to spend in the library; meaning that a program where they had to do a lot of research was bad. I don't know, I love research so much that it is hard for me to imagine that people look at this as an unpleasant experience, and I guess that is one of the things I try and do in my program is to somehow convey to the associates that they will be better off if they can learn what an exciting experience it can be to undertake some of the research projects that come along, and believe me, we get really weird research projects in our firm.

In reviewing my experience as the Library Director, I think that over the years that I have been at Shea and Gould, I am convinced that I was hired to be a custodian of the books. What I was hired to do originally; had nothing to do with facilitating the information retrieval process. I was just supposed to make sure the books were back on the shelves, and I guess a lot of fortunate accidents occurred in the time that I have been there and things have changed substantially.

We now have a reference staff of five people and a staff of twenty, so the prestige of the library has grown in the firm. I think one of the first things that happened to enable me to promote the professional contribution of the library was that in the first year I was there, a partner came to me and said, "Here is an American Lawyer article that describes the summer associate program" by, I think it was, Donna Tuke in Chicago, that had five legal research modules that she had presented to her summer associates. Then he said "I know you are alone, but can you see if you can do something."

I thought it was a really exciting challenge. I think one of the important things is to not set your sites too high. I knew I couldn't do an ideal program, so the first year I just started out doing a combination of orientation and a little bit about research, and each year it has changed and grown.

I now have reference librarians that assist me. We do individual modules and we have been really flexible and each year the program gets better.

One of the problems with planning for summer associates is that, at least in my firm, they don't all seem to be there all at one time. Maybe there is a one–week period when they are all there. So we end up having to do the same program several times, and this year we are doing it in two parts.

The day after the associate arrives, we are doing a 45–minute orientation just about the rules for using the library and to try and reinforce that there are people called librarians that you go to for research questions, and then there are the clerical staff who are very helpful but they are not your experts, and make sure you are going to the research experts.

Then we are doing an in–depth program that will cover research tools and techniques about two weeks after people arrive at the firm, because we had to deal with this problem of getting appropriately sized groups.

With the fall associates, it's broken into two parts. We do an overview of legal research and then we are part of the program for the litigation department. They have something called "Litigation School." The litigators are expected to go to school one night a week for the first six months that they are at the firm, and one of the first modules we have is Research for Litigators. The same thing happens in the corporate department; we do a special module for the corporate people.

One of the nice surprises I had this year was that we got Bob Berring's Commando Legal Research tapes, and I sent out a memo offering it to all the attorneys. Frankly I wasn't expecting much of a response, but the response was overwhelming — fifty people out of 250 said they were interested. Partners and associates! I thought maybe two or three people would respond because (as you know) attorneys are so pressed for time, I was really surprised that many would acknowledge that they would try and make the time to come to a research program.

Another thing that I think we have to consider is setting our own priorities. There was recently an article in *Library Journal* by Herb White where he says "Don't give people what they want, give them what they need." And I think it is very easy for us all to get bogged down in doing things like conflicts checking and, running the file room, and I really think the more important things we have to offer the firm are expertise and our imagination and creativity in facilitating the research process.

I also think that creating a research program will enrich your job. Don't just set out to teach what you know, make this an opportunity to go out and learn more.

In the past year, I had an opportunity to start teaching a graduate research program for library science students. I learned so much and it has definitely contributed to my abilities to a reference librarian and my ability to teach the program well at Shea and Gould.

I think we have all agreed that law schools in general are not doing a very good job at preparing people to come into the firm environment. Even if they were teaching the basic legal research, there is something so different about being in a firm. I don't think that the schools can really teach that the right way. There are a lot of pragmatic things that come up, like how do you get the actual 10k and how do you deal with the time pressures?

I think that's another part of the educational experience. It's telling me that we are working in another time zone here. We are working with different pressures. It's not just knowing where the books are, it's knowing that you have to get the answer in 12 seconds. That's what I call the hidden curriculum.

I agree with Marie Wallace. We really can't teach them all the research, but we have to teach them how big the research universe is. I see summer associates as sort of like ancient astrologers. Maybe they have a telescope, but they have it pointed at their foot.

The problem is that computers make legal research look so easy, and if they are putting together bad searches, and if they don't know all the possibilities, they will come back and say "I was looking for the Magna Carta and it wasn't on LEXIS." We all have those questions.

People come in from really great law schools and they don't know what books the federal law is in. I think that we also have to acknowledge that the law schools are not teaching them about form books; they are generally not even teaching them too much about statutes. People learn about caselaw and they learn it from casebooks. Often they don't even have to go to the primary sources of caselaw.

I suppose in some firms there is an issue of getting support for an education program. Frankly, I don't think in my firm it has never been a serious issue. I think the support is already there. I find that many of the partners, because they went to school so long ago, are totally mystified, not only by the cost of on–line legal research, but also by how is it done? Are attorneys going into the appropriate files? I find associates think that everything is on–line from the beginning of time. They don't understand that there are time limits and that there is more than one place to go. I think that a very easy approach to getting a program started, if you have that problem, is to simply talk to the partners that have come to you with the LEXIS and Westlaw questions — "Why did this cost $12,000? My client doesn't want to pay?" I think that is a really good way to begin gaining support.

I recently had a partner come in, who said, "It cost $2,000 to cite check a brief. There is something wrong here." So I'm having him to speak in my introduction this year; He is going to come and talk about why the legal research program that the library is running is important. I think that is another important way of getting credibility — to have a partner come and say, "This is important."

Has anybody really had a problem with getting a budget for putting a program together? I think that you can put together a decent program with almost no cost. What do you have to consider? The biggest cost is your time. You have photocopying, you have typing, but if you look at the amount of money that they are pouring into the summer associate program, entertaining these people, your program is going to be about the same cost of an appetizer at Lutesce. As you know, many large firms are just throwing money at the summer associates. I just don't think in that sort of environment you are going to have a problem getting them to foot the bill for something that is a little bit educational.

In terms of getting your program credibility, I think that the program should not be optional. It has to be mandatory. And over the years, I've had the problem of people coming for the research program and then getting a phone call from an attorney saying, "You are going to a deposition now." I think the best way around that is to send the partners a notice ahead of time about who is going to be attending the program and why it is important for them to be there. I have found that has really helped.

I also think that it is important for your program to be announced as part of the overall CLE program or recruitment process. The problem with some recruiters is that they come up with these really dippy names for the library research program, and I feel that I have to control what my program is called because she makes it sound silly. Psychologically, you have to make it sound important and compelling for them to attend.

Another thing you have to consider in preparing your program is not to set your sights too high and not to be afraid of making mistakes. Over the years, my program has evolved, and there are things I have taken out. I realize that there were times when I was definitely putting people to sleep. But I have learned from that, I've learned how to read people's cues — that they are getting bored, they are fidgeting and their noses are about to hit the conference table.

Another technique we have tried since I have the other librarians participate is we alternate speaking. Each librarian speaks for about 10 minutes on a particular topic, then another librarian might interject a comment and we get people to ask questions. We also ask the associates questions as we go along, and it has definitely become more of a participatory seminar experience.

How do you decide what the associates need to know? Of course you look at your firm's practice areas. I think it is also important to consider presenting materials you are comfortable with. I frankly have no intention of talking about the EEC any time soon. I just am not comfortable with that subject at this point and there is no urgent need for it. Also, identify the materials that they are going to be using regularly. As I said before, an associate has never seen a form book, and they are a pretty common commodity in actual law firm practice.

In the handout, I have listed a number of topics that I use as modules in my program. Among them are definitely state practice materials. Then there are peculiar things, for example, New York does not have a code of evidence, and of course, somebody could spend hours looking in McKinney's for the section that has evidence and it just "ain't" going to be there.

I also highlight state legislative history, state and federal administrative law, and computer–assisted research. We really feel it is possible to educate the associates to become effective researchers by recognizing the importance of time constraints. All too often associates have gotten an outrageous question and sit on it for two weeks and then come to the library and say, "I need everything on IBM." Or they will run it through NEXIS® all without asking us, "Is there a better way to do this?"

I think it is also appropriate to consider teaching them just the basics — how to use the digest, what are the sources of case law and statutes. I think it is important to give them your firm's guidelines for using LEXIS and Westlaw — what is appropriate to print. Teach them how to use segment searching, how to use these systems more efficiently.

Most of them are unfamiliar with looseleaf services, so we do a little module on how to use a looseleaf. I'm just going to teach them one important thing (like, in CCH, you are looking for paragraph numbers, not page numbers) because even when you teach them these things, they will at least come to you and say, "I'm having a problem with this and I know you are an expert on using these materials."

One of the things I think they are very surprised by is that authorities don't all agree with each other. That really blows their socks off because they have come out of law school thinking they can absolutely find a coherent and consistent rule of law for each issue. They will know nothing about document retrieval, what to do if a partner asks them for an annual report or something like that. I think it might be a good idea to give them checklists for performing legal research.

I see the same questions coming up over and over again, and I think it is time to consider giving people guides. I am going to talk a little about pathfinders in a few minutes, and I think that a good way to leverage your reference staff is to have them put together what they already know about this type of research and make it available to the attorneys even when we are not around.

Another thing I think is important is to acknowledge that there are in-house resources not limited to a brief bank or memo bank. People are resources. For example, there is an attorney staff who helped write the equitable distribution law in N.Y. I am sure that everybody has experts within their firm who are often the best people to go to if you have a question on a particular type of issue.

Another thing that brief banks are good for is identifying someone who already performed research on a particular topic that they can go to.

I also give a little attention to teaching the associates secrets of a reference librarian and what my favorite reference books are, for example, the New York City Green Book. I think it is important for them to understand that New York City has a mysterious legislative process. It's amazing that in a city in that big, a city where corporations from all around the world operate, it is extremely difficult to get at the laws. I can't believe that nobody has complained until now.

In terms of making a great presentation, I think it is important for you to love what you are doing and show that to your audience. You have to believe it is important, and if you don't believe what you are doing is important, they are not going to believe it.

As I mentioned before, you have to get the associates to talk. One of the things I did last year when we opened the program is that I asked all of the associates to talk about their experience with research, either what kind of research program they had in their law school or what work they did on a special research project to gain some sort of expertise. It was really shocking. We had 50 summer associates, and only one of them admitted or acknowledged or recognized that he had done any sort of specialized research. Most of them thought that LEXIS and Westlaw training was the legal research program at law school. They didn't have any recollection of doing any thing more than that.

I think that it is also important to get them to recognize that you are their ally. You are going to help them look better. Again, it is safe for them to ask us any question, that no question is stupid, and I think it is also important to give them some sort of a warning about what can go wrong. It seems that every summer we have a summer associate who runs up a $5,000, $10,000 LEXIS bill, and then in September, the partner comes in screaming and blue and wants to know what went wrong. I think it is better to give them a sense that this environment is a little bit different than law school and they have to learn how to work within our parameters.

Also when you present your program, I think it is very important to start with some type of material that you are really comfortable with and recognize that you are not going to be able to teach them every facet of this research. Just pick out one major point and emphasize it at the beginning and at the end and if they learn that, you will have run a successful program.

Another thing I think is important is to use anecdotes from your experience about the types of interesting questions you get. You have to teach them to communicate with partners, because sometimes they will be sent down with the wrong information, and these are not people who are prepared to challenge the person giving them an assignment. So, of course, they are not going to frame it as a challenge, but they should find out how good the information is. When he says it was five years ago, was it really five years ago, could it have been ten years ago? When he said that the store was involved, was it Saks Fifth Avenue, could it have been Bonwit Teller's? Sometimes, people give associates facts and they are not really sure how accurate their facts are.

Another thing that we often talk about is just how far do you have to go? I suppose it relates back to that thing about, if they ask you for eggs over easy — is it your job to get it? But some of our reference questions are that weird. We had an associate come in a while back who had to know how much a race horse eats. We handle those questions, and I want them to know if they get a question like that, they can come to us and they shouldn't even try to tackle it on their own without getting a little bit of expert advice first.

I am also now convinced that I don't want to be doing the library rules and regulations at the same time that I am doing the research module. In the future, I won't do them in the same program because it dilutes the importance of the research program.

On the question of audiovisual materials, I try to avoid them. I have tried to use overheads and they always confuse me. I can never put my pencil in the right place, and I forget what I am talking about. I think this summer for the first time I am going to use a pad and try and do some interactive things with writing on a board, but it has taken me four or five years to get comfortable doing something that interactive.

I think it is important to give them a handout, give them something that they can write on, but as other people have said, don't give them the whole package up front. I found though that after the first time I gave new associates a manual was when I knew the idea of the program was a really a success. A second-year associate came to me and said, "We never had a research program; we never got a manual. Do you think you could do something like that for us?" So I think there is a need out there.

I haven't mentioned the idea of training partners. It's something we really have to think about, not that they are going to show up for a classroom sort of educational experience, but I think it is important to communicate with them about what can go wrong with legal research. They want to know about new developments and as someone said yesterday, the newsletter is a good way of communicating with them.

Also, I am considering working on a very in–depth memo which describes my observations about the problems and challenges of legal research as it exists today, and try and get them more comfortable with supervising the research of the associates.

A lot of you have seen Ellen Callinan's article on the reference process, and one of the things that struck me was her discussion about using a pathfinder. As I am sure you all know, a pathfinder is just something that you would write up as a guide to how to perform the research on a particular topic. I have a handout where I describe the source of materials I think would be useful to include in a pathfinder.

In terms of how much detail you want to put in, it depends on your time and the philosophy of your firm. Do you want to tell them the exact section numbers to go to for this topic, do you want to give them the names of all the landmark cases? It is really a question of balancing your time and your philosophy about how you want the research experience to progress. But I think it can be an important tool because it empowers the associates to continue the research process on their own.

It also suggests to them the vast numbers of possible research avenues they can take in pursuing a question. I find that often the associates have very limited expectations and they give up quickly on a research problem.

It seems that every summer we get several questions on the New York City rent control laws and these are almost impossible to do research on; you won't find your best materials in any of the traditional sources. One of the most important sources for this kind of research are newsletters that cover landlord/tenant law in New York City (there is next to nothing in the New York Digest Third).

So again, one of the first things I look for when somebody comes with a research topic is a newsletter on the subject, because that's where you get the best coverage. I have come to believe in the past year that no topic is too specific to be the subject of a newsletter. For instance, did any of you get the Alaska Oil Spill Law Reporter? Captain Hazelwood was still hung over and this was on my desk.

I think another thing we have to teach them is a little bit about how to use the telephone. All of their answers are not going to come out of books.

I just have to mention this. Last week we had a question — the attorneys said they found out that an expert witness was abducted by aliens, (this question didn't even come from the California office). The bare part of the problem was that the article was in the *Globe*, not the *Toronto Globe*, but the *Globe* that you see on the supermarket stands. The reference librarian said, "We called the *Globe* and they don't have a subject index, you have to know the date it was in the *Globe*." The staff was ready to give up, but I can't give up on a question like that. All this starts percolating through my head and I'm saying, "Who knows about aliens?" Those people who are on TV, on "Geraldo" or "Inside Edition" — there are always these people who are obsessed and know everything about every time aliens landed. So, I said, "Go to the *Encyclopedia of Associations* and find someone who is obsessed with UFOs." They called, and they got a guy who said, "OK fine, where did the space ship land?" and he called back a day later and gave us the cite to the *Globe* article and we got a copy of the article. I think the lesson here is that you can't be too proud. I would love to think that I am always doing research in the British Museum, but I "ain't" you know.

In closing, my philosophy in educating the attorneys is simply to get them to acknowledge the size of the research universe. I think that when they come into the firm, most of the resources are invisible. The most important thing we can do for them and for our firm is to suggest the magnitude of the options available to them, and I think then we are doing a good job.

Did anybody have questions?

Q: [Inaudible]

A: Yes, that's a very good point because I have had attorneys come to me and say, "Well, I have already called the other side." Your eyes are spinning in your head and you wonder, should he tell the partner, is he going to be here next week if he tells the partner he did it? I think that is a good point to raise — that they have to be very careful about who they contact because there are a lot of sensitive issues. But I generally will call an intermediary to make the phone call for me if I think there is some area of sensitivity.

Q: [Inaudible]

A: We hold them in conference rooms and they vary from one hour to two hours.

Q: When do you schedule these classes?

A: It depends; most of them are scheduled in the morning and we did the Commando tapes after work and people came for that. I would like to have done the Commando tapes at lunch but we now have a conference room problem, so I can't really get a conference room every week at lunchtime, so some of them are after work.

Q: What topics do you include in your handout?

A: Guidelines for how to use LEXIS and Westlaw, sample segment searches, my favorite New York practice books, my favorite reference books, something about business databases and the kinds of information we can get out of business databases. Also what else I put in the state statutes that are online — UCC filings that are online. Library map, a library staff directory, what we do in the library, who does what.

Q: When you put that all together, do you spiral bound the whole thing?

A: We have been velobinding, but this year I want to do a spiral bind.

Q: All in one piece?

A: Yes.

[Gitelle] Our next speaker is Stephanie Heacox, the Online Services Librarian at Sullivan and Cromwell in New York City. Stephanie manages the online database services and CD–ROM products at her firm, and does training and support for all those various data bases.

She's going to discuss online training, how and where it should be done, and what your reps can offer in terms of support, material and resources.

Stephanie Heacox

As I watched the various presentors over the last couple of days, I felt compelled to rewrite everything that I had — first, because I didn't have enough humor, and second, because I didn't have enough time. Unfortunately, there's nothing I can do about the latter. In contemplating how to impart unto you my knowledge, experience and adventures in online services within twenty minutes, I was reminded of a summer course I took as an undergraduate. It was basically a history of music from Gregorian chants to the present day in six weeks. I hope you retain more from this experience than I retained from that.

I'm going to try to cover a lot of nuts and bolts issues, little strategies that I've used to accomplish my goals. There is, undeniably, a lot of maneuvering you must do through the jungle of office politics, and I have developed some basic rules which will be outlined in this presentation.

Basic Rule Number One is that politics are necessary evil, and it is exceedingly important that you know the politics of both your own firm and of the vendors you are dealing with. Corrollary Number One to this rule is that fear is a tool, and should be exploited. Corrollary Number Two is that competitiveness is also a tool, and should be exploited. Basic Rule Number Two (which may come first in many peoples' minds) is that money, the bottom line, is always a valid issue, to be raised whenever possible.

I'm going to employ an interrogatory format which has been used effectively by several presentors.

WHO? I'd like to begin by discussing who it is we will be training. We've covered this in relation to other aspects of legal research, and I think that most of those considerations apply to online training as well.

Obviously, we are going to train our attorneys. We will focus on training new attorneys and summer associates first, but we should not disregard the fact that lateral hires, senior associates and partners may also gain from online training. Their training may not occur in a classroom setting, but rather in specialty seminars or individualized training sessions. We should be concerned with retention or updating of old skills as much as the introduction of new skills.

Paralegals — I think that we covered that area pretty thoroughly the other day, but I want to emphasize that you should not overlook paralegal training. If you examine your LEXIS or Westlaw bills, you may well find that a large portion of your paralegal staff is doing more searching than your attorneys. And they're doing major projects which require extensive online searching and printing, so it is really essential that they understand how to search well and how to control costs.

I would like to include in this discussion a group which hasn't received much mention so far, namely, library support staff. Its very important that they be able to run some basic searches because, when an attorney walks into the library, she often directs her question to the first staff person she sees. There are many basic reference requests which support staff might be able to answer, for example: "I need this case and the reporter is off the shelf," or "I need this no–action letter;

here's the cite," or "I need a copy of this *New York Times* article." I think most of us feel confident that many of our support staff could field these types of questions. In addition, since we are all aware of the (abysmally low) salaries drawn by most support staff, online training can be a real benefit. I know that in our case, many staff members intend to go on to law school or library school, and online skills are very valuable either place.

As for other support staff, unlike print resources, I do not recommend giving training to literally everyone in the firm. There is generally very little call for secretaries or other clerical staff to perform online searches, except in very special circumstances, so I will not be addressing this issue.

WHAT? The next question is, what databases will we train people on? At Sullivan and Cromwell, we have access to approximately 16 databases, the majority of which are not used directly by attorneys. We intend, insofar as we can, to keep it that way.

LEXIS and Westlaw are obvious choices — we train all incoming associates on both of them. I feel very strongly about this, because both services are useful and each has its own individual strengths. Inevitably, attorneys who have insisted on only learning one service (no matter which one) will find themselves in need of the other.

Databases like Dow Jones are trickier. Dow Jones was a real bone of contention at my firm. I was not enthusiastic about giving attorneys access (for reasons which will follow), but was overruled. Thus, I have proceeded as cautiously as possible.

A major problem with Dow Jones is that it is simply not as user-friendly as either LEXIS or Westlaw, and attorneys do not realize this. They expect useful error messages; they expect the operators to work in the same way; they don't know "dot commands" and they don't want to know! It is very important to emphasize that they will have to apply themselves a bit more to use this service.

Another problem is that Dow Jones has a lot of fun, "toy" aspects to it that can be very hard to control. You will find attorneys logging on to check their investments, other staff checking out sports scores and movie reviews. I have found two small ways to deal with this problem. First, since I provide Dow Jones training myself, I limit it only to basic search techniques in certain files, without elaborating on the database's other features. Most users never need to venture beyond the basics, anyway.

For the more adventurous users, who recognize that there are indeed entertainment and investment databases on Dow Jones, monitor their usage. Even more importantly, make it known that you are monitoring usage. On Dow Jones, it is relatively easy to spot flagrant abuse, because the database names appear on the bill.

For other database vendors, on whose bills abuse may not be as clear, you must depend on subterfuge. Simply make it clear that all usage is monitored — most users have never seen a bill and really don't understand what you can or can't discern. Most are convinced that you can identify every search phrase they use; it can be helpful not to disabuse them of this notion.

Additionally, with virtually any database training, emphasize cost. I really think that you have to put the fear of God in them — not so much that they will be too afraid to even use the database, but enough so that they will be reasonably cautious.

I feel very strongly that those databases which do not have the capability of recording (preferably requiring) client and matter codes should not be made available outside the library. We have 13 or 14 databases which are limited almost entirely to library use. There are occasionally specialty databases to which small practice groups may need access. Our banking paralegals, for example, have their own CD-ROM, which includes an online service as well. It has very specific kinds of bank data which we would not get questions on; the banking paralegals receive those requests directly.

Dow Jones, which at long last has the //LOGIT command, does not prompt you for that function, so when we wrote the batch file that logs a user into the service, we included the command as part of the file. When a user logs on, "//LOGIT" prints out automatically and waits for a response. Luckily, most of them don't realize that if they just hit RETURN, it would log nothing.

However, there are still a couple of rules you have to follow. You have to insist on training — just because they are using a service doesn't mean they know what they are doing. Training should still be coordinated through the library, because it is an effective way to keep a handle on the situation.

You must also insist that one person, which in our case is usually me, knows how to use all of these databases, at least for basic searching. This is to insure that if, for example, both of our banking paralegals are out one day and a search needs to be done, someone in the library will know how to do it. You can't have access to an important database without backup.

In general, we try to keep database expertise in the library for several reasons — cost is a big one. This is where fear is a tool.

Partners can be reached, as was pointed out earlier, in several ways. One of the most effective ways is cost. Give them an idea of what happens when someone who doesn't know how to do a proper search runs up a bill that impacts on a client to some hideous extent. I have some wonderful horror stories that I save for these occasions — they definitely make an impression. Especially right now, when many of us are looking at an atmosphere of increased fiscal austerity, these arguments go a lot further than they used to.

Additionally, controlling databases within the library is a very good way to increase the perceived professionalism of your staff. Do not hesitate to exploit the fact that computers are still a relatively mysterious thing to a lot of attorneys. They're still a little frightened of them, although this is happening less and less. We certainly have more computer–savvy attorneys than before, but you know something they don't know, and you have to use that as a tool to emphasize your own professionalism. Let them know you are an expert and that they should be coming to you for assistance and answers.

As far as our firm is concerned, this works extremely well. I feel that I am on a very even basis with the attorneys — I think they respect my skills as I respect theirs and that they feel I am as much a professional as they (insofar as one can do that in a law firm setting).

WHEN? When are you going to train these attorneys? Other people have touched upon this — train attorneys and staff as soon as they arrive, and make it mandatory. In the last couple of years, we have developed a new approach to respond to the serious problem of getting people to attend training classes. The difficulty exists, in part, because on day two, when a new associate is on the job, they already have a stack of assignments on their desk, and they are more worried about getting an assignment done for a partner than they are about coming to your research session.

There are several different tactics that you can apply to this and, again, fear is a tool. Associates fear partners, so what you need to do is get the backing of the highest-ranking partner you can, or the partner who has dominion over them. In our case, we have a partner in charge of recruitment who sends an introductory memo to all new summer or fall associates. Part of that memo states that LEXIS and Westlaw training will be provided within the first two days as part of the regular orientation process, and that all associates will attend. When *he* says they will go, they will go.

It makes a huge difference. We've also struck a bit of a deal with our other attorneys that the first two days of an associate's arrival are orientation days, and they may not have use of the new associates during that time. By and large, this does work. We have only used this technique for the last couple of years, but the response has improved immensely. If you get to the new associates before other attorneys can nab them, you're in good shape.

It also helps to require training or testing before they can get their password. Do not allow them to get a password until they know what they are doing, and stick to your guns.

What I am running into more and more these last couple of years are new attorneys who, for a change, have had training before. They've gone to some of the spring training programs, or they've had training in law school, and they will tell you, "No problem, I already know how to do this, just give me my number and let me go."

The problem is that many times, previous training has been inadequate, so I have developed a technique for dealing with it. I developed a short, five-question test for LEXIS and Westlaw which takes only a few minutes to answer. If they can answer the questions, I give them their user number. Most associates just blanch at that point, walk away saying "never mind," and attend the training session. In the three years I've been using this technique, I've only ever had one attorney take the test. He passed with flying colors and I gave him user numbers with my blessing.

It also helps to have a set time for training every week for both LEXIS and Westlaw. Training is always at the same location, and a sign is posted which notifies users of training schedules. Even if there is no one to train, they will sit there among the computers and offer assistance to users. Since people know that they will be there, it can be a very useful customer service and educational tool.

WHERE? The big question is where are you going to do this training? I have some prejudices here. Off–site training can work, and in some cases it may be the only option available, but it has inherent difficulties. If you can set up an on–site training program, it can be very useful. I have some hints as to how you can obtain the necessary space and funding to accomplish this.

First of all, I will also mention that I don't recommend doing LEXIS and Westlaw training yourself. Some people feel comfortable doing that, but I really don't have the time. I'm also not sure that I would really enjoy reciting the same basic search techniques week after week — that's what my LEXIS and Westlaw reps are paid to do. You should not hesitate to ask them to do this; I would be appalled if they were difficult about providing a reasonable schedule of training. Training is a part of their job, and if you were to encounter resistance, I would say that it was time to go to their supervisor and argue that an unwillingness to train users reflects badly on a product, and that you are ready to look at a competitor. This is where competition is a tool — use the competition between services where you can; it can only benefit us.

Hints for on–site training: first, find out the vendor costs involved. Now for LEXIS and Westlaw, training is free, but some companies have pretty bizarre charge schemes — Dow Jones, for example, will charge us around $100 if we go to their training center, but if they come to train us, they don't charge us at all. This makes no sense (even though I will remain silent because it is in my benefit), but the general rule is to ask, because sometimes you can be in for a surprise.

Small firms, especially those located in remote areas where there may be only one or two other firms nearby, may want to consider doing joint training sessions. If you can come up with the facilities to do it, pooling your resources and having groups of attorneys come to different firms on a regular basis for training may be more persuasive than asking a rep to come in once a week to train just one person.

Here are some arguments to make to your decision–makers for setting up an online training center. Again, we're coming back to cost as an issue — the bottom line always argues well.

Give them examples of what a bungled search can cost. Really bring it home to them how much money you're spending online and how much money you *should* be spending on online. It makes a big difference, especially in a firm our size — we're talking huge numbers and waste is a very effective argument. There's another cost that I think partners may fear even more, and that is the cost of bad answers. You must put the fear of God in them — what happens if an attorney does a search incorrectly and uses that answer in a case? That is a very serious problem which scares rather effectively and really brings home the importance of research training.

It also eliminates travel time, so your attorneys aren't spending an extra hour or two of billable time going back and forth to the training center.

In addition, the training sessions themselves can be more tailored — they're quicker because that person knows your firm, it's generally a smaller group and they can move them right along, instead of having to sit through a bunch of people with very varied interest and skill levels.

Lastly, the training room can be public access when it is not in use for training, so that gives you an outlet to put attorneys, especially, say, 75 summer associates who will need somewhere to go to do their research. Our library can't absorb that many and this is a great outlet for them. The room can also be used by other departments — it can really help to think this out ahead of time and band together to make a joint proposal. For instance, your word-processing department, if it is PC-based, can use this room for their training. Our PC Support Department, which trains on different hardware, software and internal database issues also uses this room on a scheduled basis. Our Telecommunications Department has training software which is PC-based, so they can actually do their training in this room as well. And all of us joining together and making this argument makes it sound a lot more cost effective. This is not going to be a room empty most of the time; it's going to be used.

Specialized Seminars. Your reps can often arrange for you seminars in particular subject areas — it's a really good idea to utilize that if you can, because this is where you can start to educate your partners and your senior associates. When someone from Mead will be visiting New York, I usually get a call from my rep saying (for example), our security specialist is going to be in on these dates, can you set up a special meeting? It helps to do one of two things with that special meeting. Either put it first thing in the morning, so you corral all those attorneys before they get to their offices and you can't get them back, or if you're lucky enough to have a specialist in town when there's going to be a departmental luncheon (which we have generally about one a month) you can coordinate a presentation with a luncheon. You will have a captive audience, and that's what you want.

There are some very important things about specialized sessions that you have to know, though. Know who's doing the session and, if at all possible, get feedback on them ahead of time, because your reputation is on the line. If they're no good, that reflects on you.

From the other side, if you're going to organize something like this, please make sure that people come. I organized a special tax seminar about two months after I began at S&C. I did everything right, I sent out the memos, I got the conference room, I had everything lined up. Two people came. This guy came all the way from Dayton and two people showed up! I recognize that that was because I didn't know the politics of the firm and I hadn't realized that the memo had to come from the tax partner, not from me. They didn't know me, and they weren't concerned about attending. We did it again a couple of years later — the tax partner sent out the memo, I had 28 people come and they all loved it. So politics makes a big difference.

In closing, I'm going to show you a couple of things that I brought just because we were talking about what we can get from vendors. Vendors have many useful attributes. They can do things that we don't normally think about — for instance, they can do seminars on subject areas without even necessarily mentioning their products. There's a product called Legislate which many of you are probably familiar with. It's a federal legislative product. Well, Legislate runs seminars on the Congressional legislative process among other things, totally unrelated to their product but very useful.

They also do things such as publishing a glossary of congressional or legislative terms. They also put out a wonderful guide to Congress that is so wonderful ours has been stolen and I could not bring it today!

Other vendors do the same thing. On–line publishers put out a lot of information that is mostly free and is very useful. Don't be afraid to ask for multiple copies, because these are their advertising and marketing tools and they're happy to give them to you.

Disclosure puts out a guide to SEC filings, which I'm sure most of you have seen. I hand out lots and lots of these; they're wonderful. Disclosure is happy and we're happy.

There is also a federal information primer that the Washington Service Bureau puts out which explains all sorts of governmental filings. Little blurbs on filings, certain banking filings, for example, that I don't necessarily know a whole lot about. I refer to this little book often. So utilize other tools you can get from your reps, because they're all too happy to help.

In closing, and I will close: Remember that a primary reason for bringing research functions into the library is to enhance our professional prestige. Use that. Know the various databases that you have access to as well as you possibly can and advertise that expertise. Then produce consistent, quality results in training, research and advice.

Q: Could you please list the databases that your firm has access to?

A: LEXIS and Westlaw, obviously; DIALOG; Finsbury/Reuters (whatever they're calling themselves now); Wilsonline (which I admit I use about once a year, but it doesn't cost anything to keep, so we do); Nikkei Telecom, which is a Japanese newswire (in English, but you could get it in Japanese if you wanted to); Legislative Retrieval System (LRS), which is New York legislative information; Legislate, which is federal legislative information (they both work a lot the same way); IDDIS and SDC, which are mainly used for merger and acquisitions and corporate issues; OCR, which is an export regulation database (that's one of those special databases that I got for an attorney who wanted it for just one client, and the client was willing to pay for it); Dow Jones; Newport (the specialty banking database that I was talking about); CCH Access for our tax people (not heavily used yet, but may be in the future, to cut down on printing costs); Bechtel and Disclosure document ordering systems (for SEC documents); Information America, which we use for Secretary of State filings and for ordering of documents (certificates of good standing, etc.); and last, but not least, is a service called Easynet, better known as Infomaster (through Western Union) and Iquest (through Compuserve).

Easynet is a company I used to work for, which is why I am aware of it and use it as an additional online source. In a nutshell, and I'm sure people will ask me about this later, a group of people created an interface so that literally anyone with a computer, a modem, a telephone line and a credit card can log in and do database searches on over 900 databases from VuText, Dialog — about 16 different vendors. They created a menu system, which helps users to choose a database (even though some of these people don't know what databases are) and they also created a common command language. The software translates what the user types into Dialog language or VuText language, so the user doesn't need to know the syntax of all the different vendors. It also has an online help function called SOS, which allows a user to contact a reference center via the computer and ask for assistance with a search.

Q: How do you keep your attorneys from discovering what you know or don't know about their specific searches and their cost? What if they ask a specific question?

A: Well, you're right, there are instances when your cover will be blown. We hope these are instances are isolated. You do put yourself in a bit of a corner. But our attorneys, for one thing, don't see their bills very often. I mean they really don't see them at all, and the only time they are aware of them is when I point out problems to them — I go through the bills periodically just to see if someone is blowing huge amounts of money that I should know about. So they don't really come back to me with that question a whole lot because they are just not concerned about cost, which really concerns me.

Q: I was thinking in terms of cost before creating billing numbers for the client...

A: We have a log next to our computers, so in the rare instance where there is nothing yet assigned, we do that. Another really useful thing is that although we require them to put in client and matter numbers, six digits and five digits, there are leftover characters to the right of that. I encourage attorneys to use this when necessary, although generally I don't want to toss clients names onto a bill that will later be printed. In situations like that, I tell them to please put something up there that will clue them in to what they did, and that usually helps them a lot.

[Gitelle] Now we come to the high-tech portion of our program. Our next speaker is Karen Brunner, the library manager at Riker, Danzig, Scherer, Hyland & Peretti in Morristown, New Jersey. Karen does legal research classes for her firm's attorneys and legal assistants.

Karen Brunner

Thank you Gitelle. It is both a pleasure and a challenge to face this audience. It's a challenge in part because of all the presentations that have preceded me telling me how I should do a presentation. Also, because I feel that there is probably a large part of the audience that doesn't know that much about interactive video.

My topic is interactive video as a teaching tool. It could well be subtitled "the teaching tool for the M TV generation." What I hope to do is give you an understanding of what interactive video is all about and how we are using it at Riker.

When it comes to new technology, we often hear the words or the acronyms long before we understand what it is really all about. A few weeks ago, I attended a CD–ROM conference where Nancy Melin-Nelson said that if the 1980's were the age of CD–ROM, the 1990's will be the age of Multi Media Technology. Interactive video is a good example of this.

Interactive video is often described as the product of the marriage between the computer and video. It combines the very large image and data storage capacity and rapid search facility of video disc with the controlling power of the computer. It can contain the audiovisual dynamics of film, video, still photography, graphics and text, together with digital data, as a large information base which can be presented through the computer to the viewer for active participation. A simple definition is, "where the user is an integral part of the program and must make some input."

Interactive video has been used since the early 1980s in business and industry for many training programs. When I knew I was going to speak on this topic, my LEXIS representative and I sat down and did a search on both NEXIS and LEXIS. We printed out a bunch of things and weren't really paying attention. It turned out to be hundreds of pages listing vendors of videodisc products, and, by looking at it, I discovered that today there are numerous vendors putting out interactive videodiscs on topics ranging from promoting tourism in South Dakota to one entitled "Watchful Waiting," assisting patients in the decision to elect prostate surgery.

The use of interactive video to teach legal skills began at Harvard Law School in the early 1980s. Timm Hallahan, who graduated from Harvard in 1976, and several colleagues founded the program. Mr. Hallahan, who is now at Stanford, continues to be a creative force in interactive video, including the project at Harvard. In the early days, Mr. Hallahan filmed students reenacting trials on videotape. Videotapes were later replaced by videodiscs which allowed the computer to jump to any scene simultaneously. The cost of producing an interactive video lesson is very high, and many are cooperative efforts.

In 1986, Mr. Hallahan said that interactive video is especially useful for teaching practical skills that are process–oriented. Trial practice, interviewing, counseling, negotiating, discovery — all require skills that are hard to grasp by reading a book, listening to a professor or taking a text oriented computer lesson. A traditional way to learn these skills is "on the job training," where mistakes can be at a client's expense. Interactive video allows the viewer to see the skills in action and to join in.

Running interactive video lessons requires a computer, video monitor and videodisc player. By using one monitor to display the images and voices from the videodisc and the other to display the instructional questions and text generated by the microcomputer, the program can solicit and record a viewer's comments, answers and questions. During the lesson, users interact with the video screen by hitting keys on the computer keyboard to register an objection or ask a question. Each intervention causes the video to stop, and the computer asks the user to make a response, for example, citing grounds for an objection. A correct answer restarts the video; an incorrect answer draws helpful hints from the computer, which can also provide tactical comments on courtroom techniques or substantive law.

Advantages to this type of learning are many. I'm going to go over a few — I know it's going to sound like a list, but I think these are important and need to be pointed out.

The first one is the viewer is in control and can work at any pace. The lessons can take one to several hours, depending on how much use the viewer makes of the extra materials included, which could be facts, exhibits, memos or the Federal Rules of Evidence.

Another advantage is that creative thinking is encouraged by the visual and aural participation. As a result, skills are learned and retained longer because of direct participation.

Interactive video responds to individual needs, You may do a portion one day, come back and finish it another day, or maybe part of a lesson is appropriate for you and not for others. Also very important is that immediate feedback is provided.

Learning comes from inappropriate and appropriate responses. The computer is nonjudgmental and nonthreatening. A person can be alone in the room with the computer and go through the lesson.

It also mimics real time decision making situations and forces the viewer to react in a timely way. It is cost effective. It doesn't tie up the expensive time of partners in one–on–one or group training sessions. The equipment required to run the lessons costs less than $1000. The lessons themselves lease at reasonable rates. We have three lessons at Riker and pay about $495 per lesson for the year.

Training takes place on site. Finally, the most important reason for these young people coming out of law school today is that interactive video is a toy. Computers and video are things they've grown up with. They are familiar with the technology, they like it, and they learn well from using it.

Harvard continues to be the leading producer of interactive video lessons for law. To encourage wider use, they sought a commercial distributor. Beginning in January 1988, VERALEX, Inc., the electronic affiliate of Lawyers Cooperative Publishing Company, performed this job. Unfortunately, as the result of the takeover of Lawyers Cooperative by Thomson International, effective April 1990, the department of VERALEX, Inc. which included this product was discontinued. The company still provides technical and customer service support until a new distributor is found. Harvard is now in the process of negotiating with different people to find a new distributor.

Interactive video lessons are gaining more popularity in law schools where they often supplement or substitute for mock trial programs. They have also been approved for use in several states for continuing legal education training. More law firms are learning about them and using them. They are ideal for training new attorneys but are also useful as refreshers for the more experienced.

At Riker, we became involved with interactive video by chance. About a year ago, the partner who is the head of the library committee, came to my office with this clipping. It is a page from the magazine, *Insight*, including the column called, "Legal Briefing." One of the best things about it is that it refers to Nolo Press's *Dog Law*, a book which I have in my library. The item the partner was interested in finding out about is entitled, "Budding Lawyers Match Wits with Video." When I knew I was speaking at this conference, I wanted to find out more about *Insight* magazine. It was not easy to find information, but finally an entry was found in a periodical directory. It is described as a well-designed, news weekly from a conservative point of view. The sponsorship is not revealed. It goes out free to libraries but has a controlled circulation. It is published by the Unification Church or the "Moonies." But anyway, he ask me to find out more about the article that discusses an interactive video joint effort between Stanford and the University of San Francisco Law Schools. The information was not entirely correct because it states that although video has been used in business and other settings, it was the first year that it was available in law schools and law firms. I asked my assistant librarian to contact Stanford. She did call but was unable to find out anything.

Fortunately for me, several weeks later, one of the firm's receptionists called me to let me know that a representative from VERALEX was there to see me. I agreed to see him, although I was rather annoyed at the intrusion and the fact that no appointment had been made. When I brought him down to the library, I quickly told him that I knew all about VERALEX, the computer research system, from my Lawyers Co-op rep, but he explained to me that he was doing something different. He was a professional education representative from VERALEX, Inc., the electronic affiliate of Lawyers Cooperative. My hostility decreased when he told me about the videodisc lessons, and I quickly realized I didn't have to follow up that dead lead at Stanford anymore.

After our meeting, I spoke to the partner who had given me the clipping, and also the attorney in charge of our education committee. They were very interested and asked me to set up a demonstration. So we had the VERALEX representative come back just one year ago, April 26, 1989. We held the demonstration in the library. I had asked several first-year associates to come so they could try it out. As they watched the trial on screen, they were very interested in it, but they timidly sat there not objecting. The partner in charge of the education committee who was observing, finally grew so impatient he insisted that they object. The demonstration was a success.

The education committee agreed to preview several videodisc lessons. They asked me to obtain the equipment and set up a room. Luckily the firm did supply me with an IBM microcomputer and a small room large enough to house the equipment and several viewers. At the suggestion of the VERALEX representative, I contacted a company called American Technology Resources, who has provided equipment to others for this purpose. They were glad to help me out. From them, I bought a Sony Videodisc player for $499, a communications cable for $25, and a Hitachi monitor for $269. They assured me I had everything I needed.

Luckily for me, at the time, I had a person on the library staff who is very savvy about computers and good with equipment. Between the two of us, we set up the machines and tried out a lesson. Then my staff member typed up simple operating instructions for the equipment.

Finally, after several months passed, the firm decided which lessons they wanted to keep. We have two litigation and one negotiation. At the end of November, a memo was circulated to all attorneys inviting them to try out the new interactive video training capability. We also held another demonstration with the VERALEX representative which several associates attended.

But since the education committee had not set up a formal way to use the lessons and no one was using them, I suggested we arrange for short instructional sessions. So that's what we've been doing. The education committee chairman sent a memo to all associates, informing them that they would be contacted by a library staff member and would be required to come to a training session. This has been very effective.

One of my staff members conducts the sessions and they last between 15 and 30 minutes. Some of them really get into it and stay longer. Our purpose is mainly to show them how to operate the equipment, give them more information on what the lessons are all about, and let them see for themselves how it works and what it can do. At this point, we've gone through all the first–year associates and we're working on the second and third–year associates.

As I sit in the room with the first–year associates, more senior associates are outside in the hall looking in, making comments such as, "Well, when are you going to show us how to use it?" There is a lot of interest from the different groups, and everyone who has attended a session has gone away very enthusiastic.

We limit the number of participants in each session to two and find that it works best when there are two because they learn more from their interactions.

The comments from the users really say it best: "This is great, when do we get to go to court?" "The judge doesn't like me." "This would have helped in studying for the bar." "This is fun!" "Look at that prosecutor!" "I never did know the Rules of Evidence."

They also enjoy talking back to the judge and the other characters on the screen.

I will say we have had more success with the litigation lessons. The negotiation lesson doesn't allow for the same kind of interaction. But it is very well done and provides the opportunity to learn negotiation skills and techniques. I think that for the uninformed, it is most effective if they read the background material that is provided with it.

Even though they are enthusiastic when they leave our sessions, I still don't think they are using the lessons. I feel we may have to resort to something like mandatory luncheon discussion meetings where they will have been required to view a specific lesson before they come. But I have enjoyed my involvement with interactive video and it is exciting.

[Gitelle] Thank you Karen. Our last speaker is Ellen Miller, who is Director of Media Services and Educational Technology at Harvard Law School. I met and talked with Ellen many years ago when our firm was first looking for commercially produced videos to use in a teaching setting, and Ellen was the only librarian who knew anything about what was out there, how good and how bad a lot of them were. So we go back a long way.

Ellen is going to discuss videotapes and computer tutorials for teaching research and give a demonstration.

Ellen Miller

Gitelle, I feel honored that you called me a librarian. I must confess I am not a librarian but I'm happy to talk to librarians and I feel as though I get a lot in return, I feel like an honorary librarian, and I'm really glad to be here.

A few years ago it occurred to me that a conference on legal research wouldn't have had a panel member talking about video, because there really wasn't a whole lot out there on video for teaching legal research.

What there used to be were, of course, talking head videos, and we know that legal research is not a particularly visual medium. Video historically has featured trial scenes with very flamboyant advocates brow-beating hostile witnesses, but that is not quite the scene we consider when we talk about legal research. But then along came Bob Berring. He added commando researchers to our vocabularies and put some pizzazz in legal research.

I think we should remember that education and entertainment are not mutually exclusive, and as several people have mentioned, we are dealing with products of the information age who grew up with MTV and computer games. Bob and his producers have recognized production values that really can be, and should be, added to videotapes on legal research.

I've brought along a few video clips to give you an idea of what videotapes you might add to your training program and I will talk about each one.

The first one is a clip from Commando Legal Research. It's from part 6, Research Strategies. I have selected that one because in a very brief time, it is going to show several elements that make, I think, a very successful video series.

Commando Legal Research [video being played] is a seminal video series. I hope Bob isn't embarrassed. I told him I would only say nice things, and these are absolutely true comments. I think this is an important series that combines the best ingredients for successful tape.

What I want to do is give you an idea of some of the criteria for a good videotape on legal research. We haven't had a lot of opportunity to do this in this subject area, but this analysis is something you can apply to other videotapes you might be looking into for other parts of your program.

1. First of all, Commando Legal Research has an authority as host who can communicate with the audience. Communication is everything.
2. The tapes have clarity of content. They are well organized.
3. They are designed for a specific audience. In this case, there has been some small disagreement over who the audience for Commando Legal Research really is, at what level. I believe it is called Advanced Legal Research. Some librarians believe the series is more appropriate for intermediate-level legal research, but I think focusing on the proper audience is really important.

There is a wide variety of audiences using this series, ranging from law schools to law firms, paralegals and support staff, which I will get to later.

I think most programs which are designed specifically for first–year law students are not going to make it in your firms. Legal research programs designed for first–year law students who don't know where the law library is are usually not appropriate for practicing attorneys. Focusing on specific audiences within a small range is really an important criteria.

4. This series has an upbeat style; it is not boring and pedantic. This holds your attention.
5. There is humor. I think a lot of times people are very afraid to use humor. Levity in many cases adds to the enjoyment of the series.
6. It has effective graphics, some of which you saw a glimpse. That also helps to retain viewer interest. There are accompanying print materials which I have not brought, but they are an important element of a successful series.
7. This series can stand alone as a series or it can be creatively integrated into your program, and I will talk about that in a minute.

This is a hard act to follow, this Commando Legal Research, and I am going to show you something that, perhaps, pales by comparison.

CCH has just produced a new program called "An Introduction to Federal Taxes" for those of you who do tax law. The tape focuses on keeping up with proposed changes in the tax law and also keeping lawyers familiar with current tax law. The part that we are going to see follows a description of income tax regulations as found in the standard Federal Tax Reporter.

[Tax law video being played.] Here we have a bland host in a boring set who serves up scripted information. It really is a marketing piece for CCH. I can't judge whether this would be helpful to you or not. I think since you are going to get it free from your vendor, your sales rep, you might want to take a look at it and see if it is appropriate for your use, but I wanted to call it to your attention.

The last excerpt that I brought on the video side is really designed for the business community. As Stephanie indicated, the business databases are really as appropriate and applicable to attorneys as they are to business folks.

This is called "Going On–Line for Business Information." It is really aimed at the inexperienced on–line user or perhaps the technologically impaired. It takes the viewer through an actual search on Dialog. [Video being played.] Actually I like this tape and we do use it in our library because it is a nonthreatening way of showing people what data communication is about. If they can visualize what happens, then it is not some horribly mysterious process that takes place over phone lines and in a box.

I think it is a first step in orienting people. Let me just tell you very briefly about two videotapes that I have not seen and I did not bring but I know they are used. One is called "The Regulators." It is used in our advanced legal research course by Terry Martin at our library. It is a fifty-minute tape that focuses on the provisions of one piece of legislation, the Clean Air Act. It's an inside look at how a bill becomes law.

There is also an older series produced by the ABA Video Law Seminars which is called "Computers and Legal Education." Beware if you see this, only because it was produced in 1982, and things have changed a bit. Since then, the first two parts are totally outdated. The third one is called Refining Your Search Techniques, and there is a preview tape on this. It might be worth a look.

Because I am running out of time and I want to get to the computer materials, I just want to say one thing about integrating these materials into your program. Don't lose sight of the fact that there are other people at your firm in addition to new associates and summer associates who might want to learn the basics of legal research through some of these videotapes.

We ran a very successful program at our law school for support staff and administrators who had never had the opportunity to learn about legal research. The showings were over a week's time, at various times, and were very, very well attended. We combined those showings with a live librarian who was on hand to answer questions and that combination of showing videos (these are Bob Berring's videos) with someone from the reference desk made for a very successful orientation.

I'm going to turn now briefly to computer programs that teach research — not the tutorials offered by the vendors, but third-party software. These are hard to find and some interesting new work is coming out of the law schools that is appropriate for law firms.

For instance, the first thing I am going to show was produced by Professor Trotter Hardy at William and Mary Law School.

The basic lesson offers specific suggestions on research aids to solve a particular problem, and the new version, which I didn't bring, allows you to add your own information to the program. For instance, where things are in your library, where the copy machines are, where the bathrooms are, things like that.

What I am going to show you next is called "Paper Choice," and there are two versions of it. What I am showing you here, even though it is Westlaw-based, is a program on query formulation, and you can see what it covers. This was done by Scott Glanzman, who is a research fellow for CALI, a consortium of law schools, and he has done also a lesson on citators.

Let me just say one more thing. I know that there is a justifiable complaint that we are sending you law students who are not well grounded in legal research. We in the law schools are very well aware of that and at Harvard we are revising our first-year curriculum to include more emphasis on legal research.

Two of our faculty members and several librarians are developing new programs on legal research. I hope that you will see the results of our improved training when our graduates arrive at your firms.

Joint Ventures: Law Schools and Law Firm

Nora Skrukrud

The topic of legal research instruction first became visible on a national level at the AALL Annual Meeting in Atlanta in 1988. There, Joan Howland of Boalt Hall Law Library and Nancy Lewis, formerly of Cooley, Godward, Castro, Huddelson & Tatum in San Francisco, presented their findings from a survey on the then–current state of instruction. (This survey has been published: Howland, Joan S. and Lewis, Nancy J., "The Effectiveness of Law School Legal Research Training Programs" 40 *J. Legal Education* 381 (1990)). It was the first significant opportunity to examine the burgeoning suspicions law firm librarians held that law schools were not adequately preparing new associates for the rigorous research demands put upon them in the law firm. The AALL program turned into a lively debate between academic and firm librarians on this issue. No one realized, at that time, how the topic would continue to flourish, but it has. Indeed, this conference is evidence of that continued interest.

In 1989 *The Recorder*, a Bay Area legal newspaper, published an article entitled "Young Practitioners Lack Basic Research Skills." Unfortunately, my picture was featured on the front page, over the quote, "New associates don't know the first thing about legal research." One of the firm's clients called a partner to ensure none of the associates I was describing was working on his case! Fortunately since then, the discussion of the topic has gone on to more substantive, and deserving, representation.

In 1989 AALL sponsored an Institute entitled, "The Teaching of Legal Research in Law Firm and Academic Environments." In March 1990 Joan Howland and I co–chaired a NOCALL Workshop, "Teaching Legal Research: Trends and Innovations." James C. Martin, a partner at Crosby, Heafey, Roach & May, presented the partner's perspective by describing what legal research skills are required by new associates. Other topics included the impact librarians can have on in–house instruction, a debate on whether librarians can and should be teachers, and the integration of on–line tools in the teaching process.

There were numerous advantages to including a law firm partner in such a program. He supplied a listing of what concrete skills should be learned in the first year of practice, including that they understand value of support staff (read: librarians). In addition, our visibility was greatly improved as he viewed firsthand how seriously librarians consider this subject.

In preparation for the NOCALL program, we conducted a survey of 85 court, county, academic and firm law librarians to determine the extent of legal research instruction courses. For the most part, few organized programs exist. Over 60% of the firms surveyed had no first–year program, and 50% had no program at any level. Some firms, however, do have significant programs in place, and the librarian plays an active role in the design and teaching. Many firms use Bob Berring's videotapes as part of the course. Program length ranges from a lunch–hour seminar to a 40–hour program over a 4–month period, and one firm even includes homework.

One activity which has been particularly rewarding for me on a professional and personal level was the invitation to speak to Bob Berring and Kathleen Vanden Heuvel's Advanced Legal Research class at Boalt Hall. I was able to address law students on the reality of the law firm environment, focusing on the library, of course. Starting with some background on the how this topic of legal research has developed, I also defined the librarian: that is, a living, breathing intellectually curious individual much removed from the stereotype they remember from fifth grade. I warned them that the highest compliment you can pay a law librarian is not, "Gee, you're smart. You ought to go to law school." Rather, I wanted to instill in them the understanding that we enjoy our profession in and for its own sake. I then compared law school and law firm research sources, focusing on many looseleaf and reference tools they probably are unaware of. On–line sources, particularly non–legal systems like DIALOG, Information America and Datatimes, are also described, as these will be a crucial source of information in the firm. In closing, I shared some sample reference questions we have attempted to answer over the years, to give them a flavor of what to expect.

Thomas Woxland, in his article, "Why Can't Johnny Research? or It All Started with Christopher Columbus Langdell" (81 *Law Library J.* 451 (1989)) states that for teaching to be effective one must have a context in which training is relevant. There is no more relevant environment than the firm library. We can tailor the instruction to a specific research context, provide solid and consistent skills, and be seen as a primary resource.

In closing, I'd like to point out some of the attributes which lawyers and librarians share, borrowed from Jim Martin's remarks. These attributes, combined with our knowledge and skills as librarians, can allow us to become an integral part of the instruction process, whatever form it may take. Having a perverse fascination with the subject at hand, we are also careful, thorough, tenacious, organized, thoughtful, curious, skeptical, and have the ability to exercise good judgment. Borrow on those attributes, take the initiative, become proactive, not reactive, offer resources and offer to be a resource, both in the firm and in the professional association.

Developing an In–House Training Program

Kathy Morris Mejia

I have worn so many hats during the course of my career, and I have changed those hats so often, that now I think I could really make a lot of money opening up a used hat store. Then it occurred to me that what I am here to do is not to sell you one of my hats, but to share with you one of those hats.

When Barbara called and said, "We want you to speak on starting a training program at a conference for law librarians," I didn't quite get the connection.

I knew when I came to Katten Muchin, upon meeting Susan Siebers, our law librarian, that the whole of her operation in the law firm was very professional. I could tell, just in meeting her, the support, the organization, the forward thinking, and yet, I was surprised at the idea of this group wanting to branch out, so to speak, and also be involved in training.

If I could, just before I get the car out of the driveway, I'd like to give you an observation about law librarians over the course of my legal career.

I remember being in law school, and it was the early 70s. We had a course in legal writing and the extent of the emphasis on legal research was such that when I got to the first law firm where I worked, I remembered being thrilled.

This is a true story. I was so tickled. I knew the Massachusetts General Laws were the green books. And then I found out I was working in the labor department at the firm and I realized it didn't matter what color the Massachusetts General Laws were. I had to learn a whole new specialized library system and it was a shock to me.

In the meantime, I learned how to use the library and became a lover of research and writing. And, after practicing for a number of years, I began to teach a legal writing course. The research component of our legal writing course was something like an Easter egg hunt through the library in which many students collaborated in looking for the eggs.

I progressed on to the point where I was the Placement Director in the law school and remember sitting with law students and trying to convince them that a wonderful career path for the appropriate person would be to become a law librarian. I never convinced one person to look seriously into law librarianship. Now maybe that says something about my counseling skills, but I think it's also because law school students don't understand the value, don't understand the breadth of the possibilities for career choices such as law librarianship.

Some of you are lawyers, so some of you had a better experience in making that career choice. But when I opened up Under Advisement, Ltd. in Chicago, my career planning service for lawyers, I found a number of common complaints. The most striking one is that people say "I love the analytical aspect of the law. I love research. I love writing, but I can't stand the confrontation. I can't stand the lawyering anymore. What can I do?"

And so I want to reinforce and underscore for you how wonderful, in many ways, the job is that you do have. Forgetting whether it branches over into the training component, you have something very special, and in selecting career paths and designing our lives' work, we often overlook the value of what it is we have right in our hands, looking for the next step, looking to go beyond.

And so I just want to applaud you. I want to encourage you. I'm extremely pleased to be here and to have met you.

But in any case, there is nothing like the power of a good idea. We're all lovers of words and ideas and we do share a lot in common in terms of our tenacity, our commitment and our interest in, our zeal for the things that we undertake.

So in that regard, let me start talking to you about some of my experiences in starting up an in-house training program.

While I'm a very positive person, I'm also very candid and I'm going to say things that are going to seem a little heretical or unbelievable.

When I came to the firm in November, just last November, almost six months ago to the day, I was told, "Let's get a 1990 training calendar in order before the first of the year." I said, "Okay, we can do that." Let me put my optimism in context.

I had had an interest growing, although I didn't know it, in hiring and training and, really, in lawyer retention. Satisfaction in the profession. The ethical performance of our obligations as lawyers. All of these ideas became underpinnings for what I cared about, what I did in my work. And it all came together in the concept of in–house lawyer training.

So I said, "I'm going to create this position." I targeted three law firms in Chicago that I wanted to work at.

I applied at these three law firms and I'm so excited, I'm sure that this is going to be a reality momentarily. It's a tremendous idea, of course we can do this. But from all three I got lovely "no thank you" letters.

Then I saw a blind ad in the paper, in the lawyers' daily paper. A firm wanted someone for attorney training and career development. So, I thought, let me write to this unidentified firm. I got a call from one of the three firms I'd initially targeted. They wanted me to come in and interview. I wasn't sure, but I went and they hired me as their first professional training administrator.

The point of this story? I work for a wonderful firm, a very forward thinking, well organized, very involved firm. The firm had redefined its goals and decided to hire a lawyer to create the position. Yet, questions remained. What would a position like this be? Is this professional, is this administrative?

In this context, they asked me one very important question. They asked, "How do you think you would adapt to working in a job which has no structure?" I said, "I'd love that. I would create my structure." They said, "There's no job description." I said, "Fine we'll write one, we won't. It doesn't matter. I want to create this job."

There was a partner in the room amongst several partners interviewing me who was going to be overseeing the lawyer training effort. It became clear to me that this person was going to be central in my efforts and so I asked him something, a very lawyer–like question. I said, "Do people here like you?" And he said, "yes." What could he say? But he said yes and it's true. And thank goodness.

My point in telling you about my start–up is that it's so important that you position yourself in this effort for success rather than failure.

Here I was the ultimate outsider. You are insiders and in some ways that's a plus and in some ways that's a minus. But I was absolutely an outsider. I had no idea who these people were or what the faith of this effort was, or what the underpinnings were. Was it a public relations tool, was it a sincere training effort? You never know. There could be a lot of agendas for designing, creating and focusing the responsibility for lawyer training.

So I went ahead, and have been pleased and thrilled, wearing another hat again. In fact, I remind myself of Mary Tyler Moore. When I go to and from work, there's a bridge across the Chicago River. I walk across the bridge and literally, almost every day feel like throwing my hat in the air. Just like Mary did before every show. Such joy. I was, and am, so thrilled that this has occurred.

It's so wonderful to be able to contribute to lawyer satisfaction and lawyer training. Now, in that context, I went into work on my first morning, and I was taken into my office. There's no structure, there's nothing in there.

I went to read the literature and that's when, the minute you turn your attention to this, you learn about Dick.

I started reading Dick's articles and I said there is actually an industry. There is structure. There's a hotline, there's a number you can call. It's a marvelous group of people that are already involved in this. But, I said to myself, what am I going to do first? So, I said, I'll read. I'm a lawyer. I'll read and I read. They would say to me, How are we doing? Where are we? I'm reading.

Next, I said okay, I'm going to create some files, because after all the papers are going to start flying — and indeed they do — and I needed some way to organize myself. They told me there was no structure. So I'm going to create structure.

Luckily, after reading a lot of the literature, I got an idea of how to organize the process. I wanted to do an assessment process. I read about it, I saw that you were supposed to do that. So I created a questionnaire. It was logical, lawyer like. We needed information, so I created a questionnaire. I'm like the Maytag repair person. There is nothing coming back.

I took that as a message. I said, I'm not doing another questionnaire at the moment. Building credibility, fitting into what will work in your environment is absolutely essential.

So I decided to go talk to people. I said I'm going to go introduce myself to people and talk to people. I had to decide who to talk to.

I went and talked to one of the lawyers in charge of recruiting to get some ideas on who to interview in each department, and to one of the most organized lawyers in one of the best organized departments. I went to them and they gave me two beautiful lists of who to talk to.

And I went and I started to talk. My assessment phase occurred. But I shortened it.

Let me give you an example of what I learned. In one of the smaller departments, I talked to one of the senior lawyers, who someone told me was very supportive of training. So I went and talked with him and asked my questions.

What I learned was: We have ongoing training in our department. The laws change so quickly in our department, we get together continuously. The associates in our department are trained and know what's going on.

So, the partner continued, it's a wonderful idea and we're very happy to have you, but we don't need you in our department. I'm sort of relieved. I've got plenty of other departments. I'm thinking I started with a good one, they don't need me.

And soon I see one of their associates in the elevator. I was so thrilled because I had looked in the picture book and recognized this person. I said: "I'm so happy to meet you and understand that your department doesn't need me." He said, "Who told you that?" Now I couldn't tell him who told me, but I took what he said as a message. I said to myself, gee this asking, I get some answers, but I don't know quite what I'm going to do with the answers I get.

So I went to one of the bigger departments and I went to one of the associates who I'd been told was really in the know. What do you need in terms of training? We talked, I asked the questions and she told me among other things what would really be great was if I could get together a list for the department of the sub–specialities, the practice areas and circulate it so that everybody would know what was available for the possibilities in taking assignments and getting work and broadening their career base and so forth.

That seemed logical to me. So I went to one of the partners. I said, "One of the things we might do is get together a list of the sub–specialities." "We don't have sub–specialities in this department." I said to myself, well I think the list of sub–specialities is a bad idea.

The point is you want to move but you can't move too quickly and you have to definitely let go of your ideas if they don't seem right. You can't lose your energy for it because there will be lots of other ideas that will be appropriate. It's a process. It's a learning process. And listening is one of the most important parts of that process.

Being insiders, maybe you know who to talk to and maybe you know where, to use an old Chicago expression, the clout is. Maybe you know who would be the good teachers. But there is one thing that they know about you. They know you in your role. Your primary role is law librarian. And you may be visible or you may not be. It can depend.

It takes some thinking on your parts in entering into this forum. If anybody at your firm would like to call me, if you propose this or talk about this, I will tell them, "For me, this is a full–time job and when I made a proposal to sell this to a firm, I included hiring, I included training, I included lawyer evaluation. I included working on the assignment system." But I never included trying to run a law library. You've got a major job, the job that you're doing. How in the world could you take on an additional major task?

In a way it's a decision whether you want to be the one to try to initiate some of these things, delegating some of what you do elsewhere or move this along to someone else.

It certainly is a lot of work. And I can sense from this group that there's no reason to do anything, unless it's going to be done well and be done right. There's nothing worse than being part of a training program that's had certain phases in the past where people took it up and then dropped it. And that's the last thing you want to be, one of those phases, where someone can later say, well we had a law librarian doing this for a while and that didn't work.

That's not what you want. In understanding why it's difficult you might need to, in reading Dick's literature for example, understand the scope of the training possibilities. While some of them are the standard substantive training within departments or across departments, some of them are the practice skills development which are very hot right now in terms of negotiation training, trial practice and so forth.

There are many, many other things. Not only the formal training, but the one–on–one training. Helping people be good supervisors. Helping people understand how to take an assignment. Helping people revitalize their roles as mentors.

Associates, as you know, have very high expectations and very focused thinking. If something can help them now — good. All to the good. But the truth is, it's a very demanding job to take on in terms of pleasing the population. And on the other side, the partners — some of them are supportive and it's wonderful and it's important to find your support. But it's a very difficult process wrought with a lot of tension. Right now in the profession, the relationship between partners and associates is very complicated.

And when you step into the middle of that, try to do something in both directions, you just want to go slow. I heard somebody say yesterday that you've been talking about taking slow steps. It's true, yet it's important to start.

You can assess and you should assess. You have to assess and you also have to start. And that's why this concept of getting the training calendar in place wasn't so crazy. And as a matter of fact, we did. We did it by taking input, by revitalizing the training committee with somebody on it from every department.

We revitalized a lot of things — streamlined them, coordinated them, made sure they happened. We got the input from the different departments, made them focus on it, on what they wanted in terms of training, and then put it into the form of a calendar. And this calendar changes weekly — almost daily. But at least it's something that's there. And it's a message. The firm cares about this, the firm will accomplish this.

I was told too by an outside consultant that the shelf life for the first person in this kind of position is about six months. Now when I heard that, I said to myself, oh, I didn't realize I was taking a risk here. I don't do things to fail. But the shelf life concept has never really left my mind. Especially now that the six months is coming up. And I don't know what happens when your date expires exactly, but I plan to be there.

I have visions for the future, wonderful ideas. But I'm going slowly, because there's a fine line between being accepted in this role and being rejected in this role. I also think you have to think carefully about the hiring of outside people as trainers, because there's a definite feeling that the lawyers in the firm should train each other.

The partners, I think, feel that the associates feel that the partners should know how to teach what it is they do. But you can't always count on them because if something comes up, they can't be there.

And the associates, you can't always count on them to be in a training program because if something comes up they can't always be there. So we have a deposition skills program. Why weren't you there? I was taking a deposition. It's hard, it's really a hard one.

The best thing I can urge you to do is get some credit in the system for training time. It's important to get some recognition for the training time, either as a counterpart of a billable hour or recognized by some form of compensation. A bonus for the most wonderful trainer. That sounds kind of silly, but the truth is, training time has to be eased into something that matters, made something more than just a concept.

Too, be sure that it's quality programming. It takes a lot of time to ensure the people will come, people will listen, people will learn, people won't be overly critical.

To close, I brought some evaluations from a program that we ran. The range of evaluations was such that some people said it was excellent and some people said it was poor. "I thought it was excellent." "It was substantially a worthless program." "The consultant was very good." "The consultant is a charlatan." "I enjoyed the controlled dialogue moderated by the consultant." "The consultant should be taken out and shot. I hope he was cheap."

It's a difficult process but we must dare to take that leap of faith and be willing to listen, take the feedback and adjust our expectations and persevere. We have the commitment. I applaud your interest and I'll be pleased to talk with any of you who might want to work with me in the continuing effort for in–house lawyer training. Thank you.

Research Instruction: Designing the Direction

OVERVIEW

Jim Hambleton

Let me describe what we are going to try to accomplish this afternoon, and I realize a lot of people are already overloaded with information. We are going to narrow the focus with which we began this morning. This morning you heard about particular individual presentation skills. You learned how to use humor and you learned in general from watching your own videos about the ways in which you are effective and the areas in which you might need some improvement in presentation.

This afternoon we want to narrow that focus and look at how you can use those presentation skills in a law firm environment by constructing courses in a curriculum of teaching legal research. We are going to look at that from two different standpoints.

We are going to start with an overview which describes the reasons why you might need a program in a law firm and how you might structure that program to address the needs of partners, associates, and summer associates. And after we have heard that presentation, we are going to have a critique from a "reactor" panel. I found out that one of our people works for the Nuclear Energy Commission, so she wasn't sure what the word "reactor" means in this particular context. Our "reactor"panel, a lawyer and two librarians, will make comments about the presentation.

Then, after a break, we will have a presentation on research and instruction for paralegals — how research instruction can be addressed to that particular group. And, again, we will have a "reactor" panel composed of two librarians and a legal assistant from a large Washington firm.

Let me give you the cast of players now. I didn't introduce myself. I am Jim Hambleton, Manager of Legal Information Resources at Haynes and Boone in Dallas. We are a large Texas-based law firm with a little over 200 attorneys in four offices.

On my far left is Jeff Pash, who is our partner participant from Covington & Burling in Washington. Jeff has both of his degrees from Harvard and he is a sports litigator at Covington. To my immediate left is a guest star who is not on the program. Ellen Callinan wrote an article on research instruction in the law firm environment in the current *Law Library Journal*, so I invited her to be on the program to give her particular insights. Ellen has her J.D. from William & Mary and her degree in Library Science from Capitol University. She has been Library Director at Crowell and Moring for a number of years.

On my far right is Rich Leiter, our keynote speaker. Rich has his law degree from Southwestern University, his MLS from the University of Texas at Austin, and he is Library Director at Littler Mendelson Fastiff Tichy, which is a large labor law firm in San Francisco.

On my immediate right we have Connie Dickson who is Librarian at Gibson, Dunn & Crutcher's Washington Office and who received her MLS from the University of Maryland. After break we are going to switch and our partner/participant will be leaving and Helen Aikman-Whitman, now sitting in the audience, will join us as a "reactor." Helen is a commercial litigation legal assistant at Shaw, Pittman, Potts and Trowbridge.

So, without further ado, I will let Rich lay the framework with his presentation.

Richard Leiter

LEGAL RESEARCH INSTRUCTION FOR PARTNERS, ASSOCIATES AND SUMMER CLERKS

Good afternoon. I am a little nervous at having to tackle this topic. In many ways, I feel as though this is really the meat of the entire program. The outline for the conference calls this, "Designing the Direction: Legal Research Instruction for Partners, Associates and Summer Clerks." In a law firm setting, there is no larger potential group of people to whom to teach legal research. In this portion of the conference, we will examine the fundamental issues that we confront when considering why, what and how we teach attorneys and summer clerks in a law firm.

Before we get started, let me describe how I am going to approach the subject. There are two general topics that I want to address. We will first look at the issue of why we, as law firm librarians, should be interested in the issue of teaching legal research at all. In this portion of my presentation, I want to consider the issue of the so-called "crisis" in teaching legal research. We will then look at what I believe to be the imperative behind the answer to that question and then define our responsibility as teachers as librarians in the law firm setting.

Finally, I want to give you some ideas about what we should be teaching and how we should be teaching it.

I. WHY WE TEACH LEGAL RESEARCH

There are four reasons that I see why we teach legal research. First, we teach legal research to train new attorneys. Second, we teach legal research to enhance existing research skills. Third, we teach legal research for what I call "PR", or, to market our library expertise. Fourth, we teach legal research because it is our job.

A. To Train New Attorneys

Training new attorneys is the type of teaching that is probably foremost in all our minds. The reason for this is obvious. New attorneys and summer clerks are the ones in our firms with the least number of skills — they are the ones with the most to learn, and they take up more of our time. New attorneys and summer clerks are the ones who supply us with endless stories about how little law students learn in law school. In fact, it is these horror stories that have given rise to the recent concern that we have all heard about regarding the "crisis in teaching legal research." I believe that as the numbers of law firm librarians have increased, the numbers of stories have also increased, thus giving rise to the perception that there is a crisis. I personally do not feel that there is actually a crisis afoot.

We have to ask ourselves, if new attorneys come into our firms without effective legal research skills, has the academic community that originally trained them failed in their responsibility? If we look at legal research as an academic subject that has two aspects, one scholarly and one practical, and compare it to other law school substantive courses, we find that it is really our expectations that are faulty, not the training that law students are receiving. Let us look at contracts, for example. Everyone would agree that all law school subjects have both a scholarly and a practical aspect. Further, we would agree that students graduating from even the best schools, while they may have excellent knowledge of the scholarly aspects of contracts, are virtually ignorant when it comes to practical skills. In other words, while a student who graduated first in his or her class from the best law school may know all about the law of contracts, and we or she may have no knowledge about how to write one.

The lack of practical skills among law school graduates comes as no surprise to anyone. It has long been presumed that they will learn how to practice law when they begin to work either with a law firm or with an experienced attorney. Why should the learning of legal research be any different? In fact, learning legal research should be even less likely to be learned in an academic setting because even though we may look upon it as a single topic, it is one with application in several different areas. The task of training law students to be competent researchers in any law firm environment in which they happen to find themselves is daunting.

Let's face it, academics do not teach practical skills. Law practice skills are, in law firms, taught by mentoring. By the same token, legal research skills, whether we admit it or not, are taught in the same way. And law librarians are the experts in the firm who are qualified to teach these skills. I think that the bottom line on this particular issue is that if we agree that improvements can be made in the way students learn practical lawyering skills in law school, the gripe is with the entire system of legal education. Until the system is changed, we don't have the right to expect students to know more than they do now.

There is another aspect to this issue. Even in the best legal research program at a law school, it is doubtful whether a law student can enter a firm with complete research skills. Most law students have little idea of what type of law they will practice. While there are some obvious similarities between the types of legal research that attorneys perform in different areas, the sources and materials that they need to feel comfortable vary significantly. Take, for example, the Advanced Legal Research class at Boalt Hall, Bob Berring's class. While I would expect Bob to train excellent legal researchers, I would not expect him to produce expert labor law researchers, or tax researchers. In one class, only very general legal research skills can be touched upon — even if they are covered in detail. This may sound like a contradiction in terms, but I assure you that it is true. A good law school legal research class should introduce students to the fundamentals of legal bibliography and the systems of legal research, but as far as teaching the subtleties and complexities of doing research in particular practice areas such as food and drug law or banking law, I would be surprised if all the specialties could be fairly covered.

From another point of view, I would have to say that teaching too many specifics in law school about doing legal research can actually hurt the new attorney. In addition to learning practical legal research, he or she must also learn to use and to take advantage of the particular resources available in the library at his or her firm. Academic libraries, even ones with very large, prestigious collections, do not always have the most practical collections. A student who learns legal research in law school will not learn about many of the most important research tools used by many practitioners in law firms.

To answer the question of why we teach new attorneys legal research, the short answer is, we must. Part of the development and training of all new lawyers is the acquisition of on–the–job legal research skills. Until a way is devised to train law students how to do legal research in law school, and the same can be said about all practical lawyering skills, the task will be left to the firms and mentors and us.

B. To Enhance Existing Legal Research Skills

The next rationale that I want to speak about is one that is seldom addressed, but that is no less important than training new attorneys. Enhancing existing research skills is an important function of the library. This endeavor involves educating experienced attorneys about new services offered by the library and about new materials purchased by the library. It is extremely important because the materials and services found in libraries keep changing at a fast pace.

Legal publishers are constantly updating their catalogs to keep up with the market and with developments in the law. Government regulation and legislation also affects the materials that we collect. Each term of Congress and state legislatures seems to produce more landmark legislation or regulation. What's more, the courts have even been active in creating rules that are affecting the lives of our clients in ways that demand studied compliance. All of these influences create more commentary and written guidance. All of these factors demand more complex, precise and timely legal research. As law librarians, we respond to these developments through thoughtful acquisition, but how often do we think to conduct seminars, training sessions or some other form of educational program to make senior attorneys aware of these new developments?All of these developments of which I am speaking are not ground-breaking. For example, in California, like most states, we have a functional, but not very good, official administrative code. Last year, after decades of complaint from users of the code, the state finally made some changes. Of all things, they changed the name from the California Administrative Code to the California Code of Regulations. That's all they changed! I recently spoke with someone from the Office of Administrative Law and asked about the change. They had a reason that was so bizarre that I can't even remember it. It had something to do with making it easier to find in the library at Harvard. Anyway, six months or so later, this month (March 1990) in fact, the state then made another significant decision about the poor old administrative code, they decided to stop publishing it! As of April 1, 1990, the state is ceasing publication of the California Code of Regulations and has contracted with a relatively inexperienced California legal publisher to take over publication. This is the sort of thing that we must keep in mind as far as educating experienced attorneys. They will always find out about such things on their own, but usually not without first spending some frustrating time looking for something else. I believe that the attorneys for whom we work expect us to not merely keep our libraries well-stocked and up-to-date, but to keep them informed about changes and new developments affecting our library resources and materials.

Another example will serve to demonstrate what I mean about teaching legal research to enhance existing legal research skills. If you were in the business when CALR came along, we all had a tremendous task of learning about the medium, selling our firms on its utility and then seeing that our attorneys were properly trained. Now I admit that both major CALR vendors have made it difficult, if not impossible, for us to act like librarians as far as training and educating our attorneys about how to use CALR, but it still is possible, if you are willing to make the effort. At its lowest level, we are responsible for scheduling sessions at the vendors' training centers. When CALR first came to our firms, we had to educate more than just the new attorneys; we had to educate the senior ones as well. It is also a continuing process. We have a responsibility to the CALR users in our firms to keep them informed about new developments in the various databases and comparisons between the two major vendors and the many smaller ones.

As law librarians, we are in the best posture to learn about new developments in the field of legal bibliography. We learn about changes and enhancements in the field in the course of our work. Practicing attorneys nearly always learn about these things by accident, by luck or out of frustration. By continually educating them about these developments, we can enhance our position and importance in the firm by promoting our expertise. This is where the element of teaching legal research for marketing/PR comes in.

C. To Market Library Expertise

Teaching legal research can help us, as members of the law firm's administration, to market ourselves and our libraries in four important respects. It allows us to expose and show off library staff expertise; it can promote library services; it can help establish an important role in the firm's attorney training and recruiting programs; and it can help establish and nurture a support base for the library.

Everyone in a law firm is constantly working within the policies of the firm's administration to establish his or her indispensable role within the practice. Each attorney strives to become an expert in his or her field. As mentioned earlier, the librarian is, and should be recognized as, the firm's expert in legal bibliography. Unless this fact is brought to the attention of the firm's lawyers, they may simply take us for granted and think of us as merely custodians of books. Teaching legal research in a law firm setting is an excellent way to play out and fulfill the part of the expert in legal research.

Teaching legal research is also an excellent way of promoting the services that the law library has to offer. Training programs are the perfect forum for informing the attorneys in your firm about what services you can offer and for establishing yourself as the indispensable source of particular types of information. I am getting a little off the subject, but is important to constantly remind ourselves that in an organizational and administrative sense we are in competition for dollars with various other departments within the firm. We are also in competition with certain rivals outside the firm. CALR vendors' efforts to market to and train attorneys in our firms are making inroads on an important aspect of our jobs. The more that attorneys are encouraged to contact local CALR vendor representatives or customer service departments, the less they rely on us for our skills in these areas. It may sound like extra work, but making your own services more accessible to the firm enhances your credibility and can also make for more satisfying work as you are able to contribute more directly in the firm's practice and individual attorneys' research projects.

We can also increase the value of the law library in the firm by establishing a more vital role in the training of new attorneys. By pushing for a significant role in new attorney training and orientation into the firm, the library immediately achieves greater credibility with the new attorneys, and senior attorneys begin to see the library as an important resource for developing important lawyering skills. The role of training new attorneys in most firms falls largely to senior attorneys. Legal research is rarely included because legal research is often taken for granted or not taken seriously as a lawyering skill. The library can achieve a stronger role within the firm's administration by becoming a permanent part of its training program.

Finally, marketing library expertise can help you create an important support base within the firm by establishing a good relationship with new attorneys. As new attorneys come to rely on your expertise and assistance in getting oriented into firm culture and practice, you can make important friends with individuals who will one day be senior members of the firm's administration. We all know how important allies can be in major staffing and budgeting decisions.

D. Because It Is Our Job

The bottom line of the answer to the question of why we teach legal research, because it is part of our job as keepers and facilitators of the use of legal information. When we examine our responsibilities as law librarians, one thing should come to mind for all of us! We are the facilitators of the use of information in the practice of law. This responsibility must include a component of teaching about the use of legal information or else we cannot truly fulfill our roles as facilitators.

Nowhere is this principle stated more clearly and definitively than in Morris Cohen's great article, "Toward a Philosophy of Law Librarianship," 64 *Law Library Journal* 4 (1971). In this article, Professor Cohen sets out a number of principles of law librarianship. The third of these principles is, "Law librarians must be teachers of legal bibliography and of the methods of legal research." As discussed earlier, it is clear that librarians are the experts in the law firm in legal research. No one is more qualified to teach it than we are. At least, we should be so qualified. Unfortunately, there are many librarians who shrink from this responsibility or believe that they are not qualified. The fact is that by virtue of our special training and knowledge, we are qualified.

There is also a practical aspect to this justification for our teaching legal research. I believe that we must teach legal research in our firms in order to preserve our sanity. By taking this responsibility seriously, you can also reduce the amount of reference that you need to do. If you take care to train at the same time that you are giving reference service, you can avoid unnecessary repetition. You can also give your patrons extra benefits by making them more efficient. When a summer clerk comes to you with a question about how to Shepardize, you will find a willing student. They usually will not come to you with such a question unless they have a burning need. Merely giving them a result in that type of circumstance will only guarantee that they will be back with more of the same questions.

To sum up our rationale for the question of why we teach legal research, it is important to realize that we should because we must. In executing this imperative, we contribute to the health of the brain trust at the firm, we solidify and establish our importance and position in the firm, and we consequently improve the quality of our professional lives.

II. WHAT SHOULD WE TEACH?

A. Four Types of Materials We Should Teach

There are four, or maybe five, types of information that we must teach the attorneys in the law firm: (1) Computer–assisted legal research; (2) Basic and advanced legal research; (3) New developments; and (4) Library procedures and service.

These four categories in many ways track the reasons discussed above for teaching legal research at all, as we shall see in a minute.

Because CALR is talked about so much and because it comprises such a large portion of our budgets, I have listed it separately as a category of material that we should be teaching at our law firms. CALR is a complex research tool that demands a lot of attention in order to be used effectively. But one thing to keep in mind is the actual impact that CALR is having on our library program. In my firm, the average amount of use of CALR per attorney firm–wide is only about an hour per attorney per month. I believe that this is typical. On that basis, it is easy to see that while CALR is given a great deal of attention in principle, in fact, it is not that important of a resource compared with our print materials. As mentioned earlier, there are obstacles to teaching CALR effectively in law firms. Most important among them is the cost factor. It is difficult for librarians to become proficient at using CALR because every time we log on to use the systems, we are under pressure to be precise. There is little room for error at $300 an hour.

Basic legal research and advanced legal research are topics that I have combined and that could easily be broken out into two separate topics. The idea of advanced legal research is relative. What may be advanced legal research is very relative. What may be advanced in one setting may be basic in another. It is important to understand that basic research for a new associate qualifies as advanced from his perspective as a law student. By the same token, when a tax attorney comes to the library with his first research project involving litigation in state court, simple things such as Shepardizing state court cases suddenly become advanced specialized research.

As mentioned earlier, teaching new developments is an important category of legal research. Keeping experienced attorneys abreast of new developments is an important responsibility of law librarians.

Teaching attorneys in your firm how to use your library is a very important aspect of teaching legal research. It is easy to forget that this is a critical aspect of library education. Simple things such as how to check out books or how to search for materials that are not on the shelf and are not checked out are important things to know about legal research. Other things that need to be taught are particular (or peculiar) aspects about the use of your cataloging system or even how to use your catalog. Each library is different in the way that these things are done. Learning about these library procedures happens one way or another. The better job you can do about facilitating this learning, the better it will be for your patrons.

Use of your library can also be facilitated by teaching attorneys in your firm how to use various services that you offer. It may be one thing to offer an interlibrary loan program, but it is another to teach your patrons how to take advantage of it.

B. Specifics: Know Your Students

It is now time to turn to the important question of exactly what we should be teaching. That is, of course, an impossible question to answer in the present circumstance because the specifics of what is appropriate to be taught in various contexts varies greatly with what you are trying to teach and who your students are. I believe that in order to be an effective teacher in any setting, it is important to know your students. By first setting out to understand who you are teaching and why it is that they want or need to know that you intend to teach them, it is then possible to structure your classes to meet the needs of the particular group you are teaching.

By thoughtfully considering who you are teaching, you will be able to make your teaching particularly relevant. Making your presentations interesting or entertaining is really only secondary by comparison. It is crucial at this juncture to keep in mind that you are teaching in a practical setting and the attorneys that you will be teaching usually are in no need of convincing about the importance of the subject matter. When planning a seminar, orientation or first–year training program, keep in mind how your audience will be using the information that you will be teaching. Be careful to avoid being too general with specific practice groups, and avoid being too specific with general groups. For example, you can probably avoid detailed teaching about the West Digest System when addressing a class that is comprised largely of future tax and securities lawyers. By the same token, there is no need to delve too deeply into the intricacies of doing tax research with a group of litigators.

C. Know Your Firm

What will the firm allow you to teach and in what format? Is it possible for you to meet with various practice groups? Can you schedule classes during the new attorneys' first week at the firm? All of these questions and others will help you get a bead on what you should be teaching. You also need to consider how large your staff is and how large the incoming class is, in order to determine how specific you can get in your training program.

The way the firm interacts with the new attorneys and summer clerks is also important in planning a legal research class. Find out if new recruits are cycled through various departments before they are expected to specialize. In some firms, the various practice areas do their own recruiting and the new attorneys that come into the firm are expected to work with that department. These factors can help give you an insight into who you will be teaching and what they need to know.

D. Teaching Partners

Partners may not know about new resources. Many of the things that you have in the library may not have existed when they spent their time in the library. It is important to reach them with information about new materials and services that are available. This will help your relationship with them as well as make them better managers by equipping them with knowledge of where to direct younger attorneys to go to begin research projects.

Many partners may be intimately aware of what resources were needed to do effective research in their practice area twenty years ago, but may be completely unaware of newer, competing resources that have become available in the last ten years. Caution must be exercised when attempting this sort of retraining.

Many partners may have joined the firm at a time when there was no librarian, or when the firm was small enough that the idea of the librarian as a professional is still somewhat foreign to them. In the present time, they may have little idea of what a librarian does. Part of teaching partners has to do with educating about what you can do for them and for the practice of the firm.

E. Teaching Associates

New associates are proving themselves to the firm. These individuals are under a tremendous amount of pressure for the six or seven years that it takes to make partner. It takes about three years for attorneys to get comfortable in a law firm and in the library. During that time, they are expected to perform miracles of research, yet they may not be given the proper amount of formal training in the methods of legal research. Any efforts that you can provide can make their lives a lot easier.

For the most part, they need very specific instruction about where to go, what to do, and what materials to use. I think that it is also very important with new attorneys to downplay CALR. In law school and in their first experience in a law firm, a disproportionate amount of time is devoted to teaching new associates about CALR when, in fact, they will be using it very little. Many new associates come to law firms believing that they will somehow be able to do all their research on a computer. Strong discouragement will help to put CALR in its proper perspective.

Senior associates, on the other hand, are closer to partners in what they need to learn. They need to keep current on the types of materials that are available, but after four or five years, they generally are comfortable with most types of research that they need to perform.

F. Summer Associates

Summer associates just want to have fun. Let's face it, they are on summer vacation. They are auditioning the firm, and the firm is auditioning them. They are not going to be hired or not hired based on the quality of their research skills. The firm is looking at their ability to write, analyze and to socialize with the rest of the firm. In designing a research program for summer associates, pure "quick and dirty" pragmatism should be stressed. Summer clerks are the most likely ones in law firms to use the more esoteric and academic materials in your library. It is a theory of mine that partners and senior associates save all the weird legal questions that they were unable to answer during the fall, winter, and spring, and give them to the summer associates. There are usually no answers to these questions.

Another thing to keep in mind when working with summer associates is the fact that the library may be a significant marketing tool for recruiting. Your training and relationship with summer clerks may involve a significant responsibility to the firm. In this regard, it is important to stress the particulars of your collection, your library staff and the quality of service you can provide. While they do not need to become experts at doing the kind of research practiced at your firm, they need to know enough to get by, efficiently and effectively.

Finally, summer clerks need to be taught how to appreciate the real–world use of CALR. They need to appreciate that CALR costs the firm and the client money — neither of whom enjoys throwing it away.

III. HOW WE TEACH LEGAL RESEARCH

There are three basic methods of teaching legal research: seminars and classes; one on one; and through the use of media such as newsletters, bulletin boards and exhibits.

A. Seminars and Classes

Traditional classroom situations have a number of advantages and disadvantages when it comes to teaching legal research. Certain types of teaching lend themselves more to this type of teaching than others. CALR, for one, can be effectively taught in a seminar–type setting in a training center. I have found that our local training centers have been especially helpful in this regard. If you are tactful, you can arrange to schedule time in the training centers where you or someone on your staff can actually conduct the training sessions. You can also arrange to have temporary learning centers set up in your firm.

Classroom settings are also useful for other purposes. Concise, practical basic training sessions can be designed to give students important conceptual grounding in legal research principles. These settings can also be used to promote library staff and resources by getting individuals in front of the group in a position of authority. These situations are also excellent opportunities to explain and set policy to a captive audience. Take advantage of it.

Classroom settings also have disadvantages. Since legal research is a skill, it is often difficult to impart practical knowledge. Because of its artificial or academic nature, it is hard to make topics interesting or vital. I experienced this firsthand when I tried to teach the List of Sections Affected in a classroom setting.

Other dangers of the classroom setting involve the tendency toward abstracts and toward making the subject matter too broad to be of interest to the greatest number of individuals.

B. One–on–One — Reference and Orientation

This approach to teaching legal research in a law firm setting involves two different formats. The reference interview is an excellent way to work with individuals with specific legal research problems of great importance to them. In this situation, individuals are not simply willing to learn, they need to learn and usually do extremely well in picking up the material. Also, since they have an immediate need for the information, they immediately apply it and tend to retain what they have learned much longer.

I have always encouraged my reference staff to treat every reference question as a potential learning opportunity for the patron. Insightfully and reasonably applied, this philosophy is probably the best and most effective teaching tool that we have. See Ellen Callinan's recent article in *Law Library Journal* for an excellent treatment of this issue, "Research Protocols in Reference Service: Informal Instruction in Law Firm Libraries," 82 *Law Library Journal* 39 (1990). The obvious drawback is that it is extremely labor intensive, and with some of the figures that I have heard about today and yesterday about summer clerk classes of 50, 70, 80 and more, perhaps even impractical, if not altogether impossible.

Another variation on this theme is that of the personal orientation. With this method, all new hires are brought to the library for individual orientations and library tours with the librarian. A thorough orientation can last 1–1/2 hours or more and the time can be spent in a personal training program directed at the individual's needs and expectations. This, too, can be labor intensive and impractical in certain situations.

C. Newsletters, Bulletin Boards and Exhibits

Newsletters, bulletin boards and exhibits are the most informal, but often very effective training tools at the librarian's disposal. The key to making these tools work effectively is that they must contain information that is highly relevant and practical. The bottom line is, if the material contained in the newsletter is not useful on a consistent basis, it will be largely ignored. I have also found this to be the case with newsletters that contain too much trivia or that are too self–serving as a library promotional organ. A well–constructed newsletter or bulletin board can attract a lot of readers and attention. If the information is important, it will get read and will have an impact.

IV. CONCLUSION

I think that in summary, I would like to say to you all that I am confident that each of you will be able to develop and implement an effective teaching legal research program in your firm. Remember who you are teaching and why you are teaching them. With a little creativity, each of you will be able to develop the program that is right for you and your firm, working within the resources and support that you are given by your firm. Do not be discouraged by the lack of overt support from your firm. You must do it anyway. Be resourceful. Good luck.

James Hambleton

Thank you, that's very helpful. In my own situation we don't have that many libraries in Dallas. We do have county courthouses with computers and that kind of thing and you are right. The last time I was at one of our branch offices, I was in the library and a legal assistant came in and she wasn't accessing LEXIS or Westlaw but she sat down at the terminal and got into the Western District of Texas docket which is now on–line, and she printed off all this docket information. In a sense, that's really where I think our market is for legal assistants. It's getting, as you said, the nitty gritty factual information such as docket information from these courts with on–line dockets. It's much more source material instruction that you need rather than general "conceptual" instruction.

Rich, I wondered if you had any comments from your staff?

Richard Leiter

One thing that I would like to mention is that towards the beginning of your remarks you mentioned training for paralegals and staff. I think training for staff has been glossed over here. At our firm we have, as part of the secretary orientation, presentations by all management staff, including a library orientation. Information is presented that is helpful for secretaries and staff to know in using the library, even if it is simply where to go to find full text of the Daily Tax Report or just to show them where things are located. That is something we should keep in mind in all of this.

Bob

Can I second what he said about secretaries in particular? There is one approach that you can take in doing that, and I have actually done so in a legal department setting and got an incredible response. I did a 10 to 15 minute orientation for secretaries on what the library can do for secretaries. The response was overwhelming. I did it one time and after that every new secretary who ever came on board requested it. It was a self–perpetuating thing. I didn't have to advertise it as being available. Word–of–mouth advertising was quite sufficient to anybody new who came on board.

There is a whole group there that seems to get overlooked along with the paralegals. Dividends are immeasurable to the library staff just because the secretaries become very independent and self–sufficient in their own research. At the same time they start using the library more proficiently. In some cases they became very proficient at it, even more so than some of the attorneys.

L. Jeffrey Pash

I was originally asked to be on this panel by my law school classmate, Nick Finke, who I'm sure many of you know. Nick said he had called because he had been asked to find a partner at a law firm who knew a lot about legal research to appear on this panel. Nick and I were Moot Court partners in law school and we used to see how many cases we could dig up in an hour under the careful and very skilled tutelage of the librarians at Harvard who we worked with. All I can say is that ten years have gone by, Nick, and times have changed.

Really, what I should have done in law school was study not how to do legal research but how to manage the telephone. I find that I spend more time on the phone than I do in the library, which I am concluding more and more is a loss. I had made a few notes before I came in, which I supplemented as I was listening to the program, on some things that seem to me important and worth stressing.

I think that the very last thing that Rich said is the most important. He mentioned this with respect to the newsletter that his office publishes, but I think it's an important guiding principle for any legal research program, and that is keep it practical. And that is true irrespective of whom the program is aimed at. It is especially true if the program is aimed at your new people to try and integrate them into the firm, but I think it's equally important if you're working with your more senior associates or your partners.

Each person you're dealing with, whether he is a new associate, more senior associate or partner, has a different set of competing pressures, if you will, on his or her time.

From the standpoint of the new associate, there are pressures that are inherent in taking a new job. These young people are tremendously bright and tremendously energetic. They have great academic skills and can read and synthesize information quickly, but they are in a brand new environment and they're tremendously nervous. It's very seldom that a new associate comes in to a law firm and immediately feels comfortable with the environment, and as as a result, they have a hard time accepting the notion that they have two or three hours to carve out in the middle of an afternoon to spend in a classroom situation that won't be immediately pertinent to one of their projects. They are more concerned with the memo that's due here, or the partner who is calling about a brief, or the person who wants them to fly to Cleveland the next day.

I'll give you an example of what I see in our own firm. We have a committee called the Legal Education and Information Committee that sponsors seminars and workshops on issues of the type that you would expect a committee like that to address. The day the memo goes out describing the topic to be discussed at the next LEIC session, there is a large sign–up. By the time the or seminar rolls around, there is a significant dropout rate.

And it's true not just with associates. I see it with summer associates as well, who generally don't have the most demanding schedules. One of the things that we do with our summer program is to run a deposition training course and a mini trial practice course.

The trial practice course takes all of about two days for the summer associates. But many of them find that the pressure of whatever they're currently working on is too much and therefore, they can't put aside the time to do something like that. And that's unfortunate because the course involves practicing cross–examination, depositions, opening and closing statements, and other exercises that these students would find both useful and enjoyable.

So I would really stress the importance both of keeping the programs practical in their orientation and realistic in terms of scheduling. The firm will be resistant if you want to take half the associate class away for two days out of next week to conduct a program. And the people you're trying to instruct will resist as well. They will simply not be convinced that they can afford to put out that kind of time. Which is highly unfortunate, because it's a classic example of failing to make a little bit of investment at the front end which will later pay a big return.

To make this a little less abstract, let me offer a practical suggestion. I think the most effective way of teaching these kinds of research skills is one–on–one. I saw that when I was a law student. I won't embarrass him by singling him out, but one of the people who taught me a lot about legal research is sitting in this room right now. He taught hundreds of students, and I learned a lot in just talking to him across the reference desk.

The same is true at my law firm. We've got some outstanding people on our library staff and they've been extremely helpful to me and to many others. Undoubtedly, they've gotten the same kinds of inquiries from me that they have gotten from hundreds of attorneys over the years. I would suggest making a record, if you will, of common problems. You must get asked the same or very similar types of questions over and over again. It might be well worth the efforts to make a list of the most frequently asked questions over a 30 or 60 day period. If particular questions are asked repeatedly, that would indicate a need for instruction in that particular area. That's the sort of information you could put into a Q and A format, put it into a newsletter, and distribute it around the firm. Or it could be the basis of a short, focused research seminar that could be offered to incoming associates and to others on an as-needed basis.

If the questions are in different areas, for example, some are about tax, some are about food and drug law, some are general litigation questions, you could carve them out. For the tax group, you could present four or five frequently encountered research questions and problems, offer your proposed solutions and discuss them with those lawyers. The same thing could be done for the food and drug group, the transportation group, the communications group, or however many different kinds of practice areas you can efficiently identify.

It might be quite efficient from your standpoint, because there is no reason you should have to answer the same question 47 times. There are probably other things that you could spend your time on productively.

It would also tend to make legal research somewhat more efficient because lawyers would not come to you right when they are starting a project, but instead after they have taken several steps and are looking to dig a little deeper. That is really how I think the resources of the law library resources could more effectively be used.

Let me make another point, which again goes to something Rich said. Please try to teach new lawyers not to assume that computers are the answer to everything. Because they are not. They're especially not the answer when you're trying to figure out how you're going to explain some huge LEXIS bill to your client. Clients tend to ask fairly sensible questions, such as whether these problems could have been researched in a more focused or thoughtful way so that it wouldn't have cost quite so much to do the work.

Law students — and Nick and I were like this — get hooked on the computers because they were free, they were fun, they were fast. Someone mentioned the three G's, well, the computers in law school were three F's. We could go back into this little room at the back of Langdell Hall and there were three or four computers and we just would sit there for hours and consider ourselves to be real high tech guys back in 1978 and 1979.

But it does not work quite as well in the law firm environment. While those computers are cranking out the paper, there is also a tote board going as well. Young associates who are used to having free use of the computers in law school don't have a very good appreciation for when it's appropriate to use the computer and when it's not. And they tend to use them on things where it really is not necessary, and as a result, your clients get fairly high bills.

The last point that I would make is that it seems to me that people don't always appreciate how dynamic the library is. Many attorneys tend to think that the only change in the library is that the soft cover reporters become hard back editions. In fact, it's much much more dynamic than that.

One thing that our library does is to regularly distribute a list of new acquisitions. For example, my practice area is principally sports law. Whenever there's a new publication on sports law or issues that relate to professional or college athletics, books will be acquired and sent for me or other people in the area for review. That's an extremely helpful function.

It's a good service because it keeps the lawyers current on new published works, and it also underscores the point that the library is really a very dynamic place. There's a lot of growth and change. It's not just computers, it's not just new books. It's a whole different way that develops over time of doing legal research. And it means that what I learned ten years ago and what I learned five years ago has some relevance today, but there may be faster or better or more thorough ways of doing things.

I think it's important to make sure that the lawyers at your firm get that message and understand it. They need to understand that even if the techniques they know are good ones, and will generally find the answers, that the library is a changing, growing place. Through the use of things like newsletters, or speaking at luncheon seminars, you can outline in a broad sense the kinds of changes and the kinds of new or different services that you can provide and people can then come to you with more precise problems where you're really able to make a difference.

I think that basically covers the points that I had and I'll turn it over to someone else. Thank you.

Ellen Callinan

I had planned to react to the scheduled panelists rather than to add anything new to the discussion; however, I would like to make a few points about our role as research trainers in the law firm environment.

This exercise of analyzing legal research training is motivational, and, as jacks- and jills-of-all-trades at our firms, we can use all the motivation we can get! Unfortunately, the very thought of assuming yet another responsibility is practically paralyzing. I've met so many colleagues who have taken on their records departments, conflicts of interest and vast amounts of automation — as if running large law firm libraries weren't enough. Now that we've learned how much work is involved in developing, implementing, evaluating and revising solid research training programs, I wonder how we're going be able to incorporate these new techniques into our overcrowded schedules. We've had a training program in place at Crowell & Moring for three years, but now I feel panicked about improving it before the summer associate season starts.

The point I'm trying to make is that although legal research training is a crucial responsibility, we cannot walk back to our firms after this conference and change our attorneys' legal research habits within a few weeks. It'll take months to design and implement (and obtain that critical support for) the excellent programs we can, and should, offer to our institutions. Even after we establish curricula and schedules, the process of revising the programs is never-ending. The bottom line is that we have to start somewhere and we can begin in so many subtle ways. You can change the ways you perform as librarians and simultaneously affect the legal research methods your attorneys use.

My article on informal training in law firms libraries addresses this issue. I was inspired to write the article as I observed my own young reference staff cope with their insecurities and fears vis-a-vis the attorneys. I wanted to help them build their self-esteem and to make them recognize that, as librarians, they were experts. The attorneys were coming to them for advice, not to intimidate them. By reviewing classic reference techniques with the staff and by providing them with reference protocols and pathfinders, I had hoped to give them crutches to lean on until they had the confidence and experience to act as true research partners to the attorneys. At that point, the library staff would be able to conduct informal training at the point of need. This technique, which simply involves heightening librarians' awareness of their opportunities and abilities to train attorneys, is quick, effective and a good starting point for a more formal program. A sensitized library staff is the best foundation for attorney research training.

We implemented another little program this summer. At the suggestion of our summer associate librarian, we asked the summer associate committee to forward copies of all the assignments to the library. We're going to review and annotate them in anticipation of directing the summer associates to appropriate sources quickly and accurately. The extra time should give us a chance to brainstorm a bit about unusual sources and to outline the best approach to each research problem.

These are just a few examples of ways to begin a research training program. It's much better to start with a small, effective program than a huge, ineffective one. If you do it well this year, you'll have something to build on next year. You'll also gain credibility at the firm and the more credibility you have, the more resources they will be willing to provide in order to build a bigger and better program. After instituting the summer associate research training program, I approached our management to obtain authority to hire a professional librarian just for the summer. I was given the funding and the summer associates were so wild about the idea that the committee reminded me to hire a summer associate librarian this year.

My last piece of advice is to put yourselves in the shoes of your firms' managing partners for a moment and analyze the summer associate season. For three months, your law firms are selling themselves to people who, if they accept the offers, will spend their first three years in your libraries. If your firms have committed significant resources to their libraries, they have reason to expect the summer associates to be impressed. You need to remind the partners that the libraries which support *x* number of attorneys all year cannot possibly support *x–plus* the summer associates at the same level of service. Once you put your requests for extra personnel or the Berring tapes or whatever else you need to make the library shine all summer into this context, I bet most of your managing partners will gladly accept your recommendations.

Constance Dickson

My topic is Defining the Direction: Research Instruction for Paralegals. I am not going to concern myself with detailing the contents of a program. I am going to suggest procedures that may assist you in establishing a successful program.

I think most law firms have been slow to recognize any deficiency in legal research capability in their legal and nonlegal staff. Training, if embraced at all, focuses on new associates and with the specifics of a practice, such as client relations, how to take a deposition, exercises in mergers and takeovers, developing arbitration and negotiation skills. Rarely does the partnership support and encourage legal research programs for attorneys or for staff. We are all aware of the situation in our own libraries and our attempts to compensate for this lack of knowledge and skills.

Much more can and should be done to provide new lawyers with what they need, but the success of any program depends on having the full and complete endorsement of the partnership. Law librarians have to convince the management committee there is a need for training and at the same time show that the logical and best resource for this in most instances is right there in the law firm, in the law librarian.

Within our profession we are well aware of the situation. We would not be here today if we were not. Our literature is full of articles on teaching legal research and the need for it. We are talking to each other, we are talking to the already convinced and the already converted. We should be talking to attorneys and publishing our articles in the *ABA Journal*, law reviews, and in trade publications such as the *Legal Times*.

Examples of training commitments by law firms do exists. Ellen Callinan mentioned one in her recent article. Baker & McKenzie went to considerable expense to develop their legal research training program. In firms where there is strong support for teaching legal research to attorneys, you will probably also find an awareness and recognition of the financial benefits to the firm of having similar instruction for paralegals and legal assistants. The attitude for instituting such a training program will therefore be perhaps more favorable and positive and your work should be easier.

However, more often than not the following situation is what prevails in most law firms. The paralegals employed have no training and no experience. They are usually just out of college. Their pay is low and the turnover is high. Position descriptions include such terms as client maintenance, clipping and filing, and document coding. There is no track for advancement. There is no career development program and no real paralegal department. Paralegals are usually excluded from practice department meetings, rarely deal directly with clients, and are given no financial support for attending courses to enhance their knowledge of the practice area for which they are responsible.

While the situation may be somewhat better for litigation paralegals, I believe we would agree that this is what exists to one degree or another in most law firms. Articles and publications for paralegals treat these same issues repeatedly. And yet, we are told that during the next decade the economics of the law firm will produce a major demand for paralegal support, while very little is being done now to create an atmosphere that draws the best and the brightest to the profession and to develop a cadre of trained legal assistants.

There are a number of places one can start to obtain support for instituting a legal research course for paralegals. I recommend that the first person with whom you discuss training would be the paralegal supervisor. You must be aware of the possibility that the supervisor could interpret your recommendations for a legal research program as an infringement on her responsibilities or a commentary on her supervisory ability. You must also be prepared to encounter surprise from others when they learn of the law librarian's capability in the area of teaching legal research. As an example, I refer you to a rather lengthy article in *Legal Profession* entitled "How to Create an In-house Legal Assistant Training Program," written by a supervisor of legal assistants in a very large law firm, that contained not one mention of the firm's law librarian or the possible contribution by, or even use of the law library.

Support must also be obtained from attorneys, especially those who work or supervise paralegals in certain practice areas, the legal administrator, and the paralegals themselves. Frequently overlooked in this step is the library staff, and especially the reference librarians. They are, after all, a primary source of information on how paralegals use research and reference materials. The staff will have a number of excellent observations, but before you commit the library's time to developing and presenting such a program, it is advisable to make sure that you have your staff's support.

Your position and approach in discussing a training program with a paralegal supervisor and others should be a positive one. Avoid denigrating the abilities of the paralegals in order to show training needs. Stress, rather, the positive results that can be achieved. Point out that on–the–job training is fine but that a formal structure is more efficient. Stress that a more knowledgeable paralegal will be able to take on more complicated and demanding research tasks, thereby allowing the attorney to direct her attention to other matters and increasing paralegal billable hours. Describe successful programs in other firms. Show that formal training programs are a fine recruitment tool. Drawing on others' experiences, give evidences of effectiveness and of specific benefits to clients. Use the support you received from the paralegal supervisor to convince associates of its value. And cite the supervisor and the associate support to partners when talking to them about the program. Diplomatically suggest that competent and trained paralegals will reflect most favorably on and be a credit to the paralegal supervisor. Stress also the expertise, knowledge and background that the library and its staff can bring to this project.

Let us assume that your efforts have resulted in considerable support for the development of a training program, and you are now ready to prepare a formal written proposal. Use the information, the comments, and the observations gathered during talks with the various supporters. Include the discussion points that were found to have been most effective, define the objectives of the proposed program, and identify costs of materials, space requirement, and time. Include cost offsets and financial benefits whenever possible. While the approval procedure is moving forward and you see that support is forthcoming for the proposal, you should start to flesh out the training program with detail, deciding its course content and the most effective way to present material.

There are several points you may want to keep in mind. One: Know and address the needs of the firm's various practice areas. In doing so, you should be aware that success of your program depends on how relative it is to the needs and responsibilities of the paralegals and the direct value they perceive in such a program. Despite the fact that you are a self–acknowledged authority on the EC in 1992, stifle the desire to include that topic in your program if the firm does no work in this area. There will be little support for a program that includes topics of no relevant use, no matter how interesting; worse, few will attend.

Two: Include both legal and nonlegal information in your course offerings. While it is not the objective of a paralegal training program to turn out mini–lawyers, knowledge of legal principles and concepts will have to be included to enable the researcher to identify pertinent information and terms in the literature. Such knowledge will also facilitate locating relevant sources. Nonlegal research now comprises a substantial percentage of a practice area's requirements. The use of looseleafs and periodical subscriptions such as newsletters is routine. The shelf of basic reference material grows, especially dealing with corporate information and materials on international finance. You might want to include a brief presentation on how the library is set up and a review of how the catalog can be used to identify related materials.

Three: Know the educational and experience levels of the paralegals. This information will guide you in establishing the level of the training as well as the course content. This information can be gathered through interviews or at orientation or by having paralegals complete background forms.

I want to tell you about an episode that occurred to me which I hope will underline the importance of knowing the levels of your students.

The paralegal supervisor asked me to do a cite–checking seminar for 15 or so paralegals, three of whom work in litigation. She said the senior litigation partner wanted all paralegals to know how to cite–check because he had needed a cite–checker when for one reason or another the litigation paralegals had been unavailable. He had discovered that none of the other paralegals knew how to cite–check.

Most of my work with paralegals has been on an individual basis and dealt with subject resources and their uses. However, I had done cite–checking seminars and had what had proven to be an effective presentation, with worksheet materials and handouts. I also discussed content and approach with the paralegal supervisor and learned what she wanted covered. I asked her for information on the paralegals' background, most of whom were assigned to and were responsible for practice areas that require no brief preparation or cite–checking. She assured me that they were for the most part well qualified and experienced and needed an in–depth review to bring them up to speed.

The seminar was held in one of our large conference rooms and included a rather generous lunch. However great the setting was, the presentation fell far short of achieving the goal of enabling paralegals to perform cite–checking assignments. While their on–the–job training qualified them in their subject areas, they were totally unfamiliar with cite–checking. The majority lacked knowledge of the judicial system, the Federal and national reporter systems, and the components of an opinion. Expressions in their faces told me they were unprepared to understand the why and the how of cite–checking. I had to adjust my presentation as I went along, which is not the most effective way to instruct people, I am sure you will agree.

However, all was not lost. The presentation did encourage the paralegals, or at least those who were interested, to come to the library and request further help. The staff and I were able to provide adequate training, including the use of LEXIS and Westlaw in Shepardizing™, which gave them an understanding of cite–checking. This incident underscored how vital it is that courses be structured to meet the needs of both the firm and the students.

The primary source of guidance on course content is the perspective student. It is a challenge to prepare materials that will contribute and appeal as broadly as possible so that you can inform, instruct and challenge across the group without driving some away, either through boredom or confusion.

The concern is how best to structure your program when, as an example, you have 20 paralegals, 5 of whom are litigation support, and the other 15 are responsible for a variety of subjects — tax, securities, banking, pensions, international trade, environment. In addition, some have responsibility for preparing newsletters, writing speeches and articles, and doing UCC and SEC filings. Frequently, paralegals will be called upon to perform a variety of overlapping functions. One approach in such a situation would be to develop a core curriculum to cover such topics as a description of the Federal and local judiciary, a discussion on how the Federal and state legislative branches work, sessions on Federal and regional reports and codes, and citations and cite–checking. Many of the paralegals will not be asked to work directly in these areas, but it is basic knowledge that is useful and related to their own work. In addition, many of the subject area legal resources will assume the user has this knowledge.

The core curriculum could be augmented by sessions on specific topics such as banking or environmental law. The classes could be open to all paralegals but certainly intended for those who are responsible for work in those specific and related areas. Presentations should not be restricted to legal resources but as mentioned earlier should include related sources to help the research process.

The practice of law now includes and indeed depends on considerable information from nonlegal sources. Developing knowledge of these resources and acquiring familiarity with their use are necessary skills for people responsible for specific research areas. Our reference librarian tells the story of a corporate paralegal who dashed into the library and asked her for everything available on Nashua. She wanted background, news stories, directory listings, financial information, using both print and online sources. She needed everything. The paralegal had little more than the name and that the information was needed for a client and needed immediately. Then she dashed out before the reference librarian had a chance to question her further.

The librarian assumed that the search was for a specific company since this was a corporate paralegal. But on the way to pinpointing the correct company, she learned that Nashua is the name of four towns, in four different states. It is the name of two rivers, it is the name of an Indian tribe, it is the name of a famous race horse, and it is the name of a number of paper mills in the northeast, and that was what the corporate paralegal had obviously wanted. Had she been aware of the many reference sources available, she could have given focus to her search and provided the reference librarian with assistance in obtaining the additional pertinent information.

A number of teaching approaches are now available to assist the instructor in presenting the many legal and nonlegal research and reference sources that practitioners must be familiar with. The objective is no longer, if it ever was, just to provide an answer but to develop a research process that a paralegal or an attorney can apply to every research project. The standard and perhaps favorite approach is the lecture, augmented by worksheets and other handouts, with time for questions.

Presentations could also include videotapes. These can be produced in–house, rented, purchased, or obtained without cost. Many large publishers produce "how–to" videos on the use of their materials, and they are usually free. BNA and Lawyers Co–op are two sources that come to mind. Classes or training can be held outside the office at LEXIS training centers. These can deal with not only broad overviews but with specific subjects. Guest lecturers are always a good source.

Attorneys and other paralegals, specialists, and of course the librarians can all contribute to a successful program.

There are other considerations that should be addressed when preparing a training program. Classes should be scheduled so that they are accessible to as large a number as possible. If you decide to include food at these sessions, I advise keeping it light.

Adequate time should be allotted to the preparation of student materials such as pathfinders, handouts, a syllabus or course outline. Well-prepared materials will often be used as reference sources after the program is completed.

Consideration should be given to including exercises and, if so, whether they will be completed during or between classes. Exercises also require considerable time to prepare, and they need constant updating. The question of grading or rating a paralegal and the use of this information in job performance should be a management decision.

A procedure to have students evaluate the course content and teaching methods is very important. It is vital for improving the presentation as well as the course content. Evaluations can be done immediately after each class or at the end of the session. They can be written, they can be oral and they can be a combination of all of the above.

The preparation of a final report at the completion of the training program, to include an evaluation of the courses offered and incorporating student comments and recommendations, will also be a help to you. It is necessary for management to know how the program proceeded. It is a help to you, as it will underscore where you need to improve and what was successful.

In most private law firms, librarians already do a considerable amount of informal teaching. The experience and expertise are there, waiting to be utilized. You have to find the most effective way to achieve your goals within the political environment of your law firm.

In summary, there are five primary steps for the establishment of a training program: obtain support for the program; prepare and submit a formal proposal; develop a core curriculum; set up classes, prepare materials and obtain instructors; and finally, evaluate the process and the results. The bottom line, however, and one requirement for instituting a paralegal training program is obtaining management endorsement and commitment to its establishment and success. After management recognizes the benefits that would accrue to the firm, it must then put its considerable, persuasive weight and whole-hearted support behind the training program. Such endorsement will encourage associates, summer associates, and paralegals.

Enjoy the rewards from establishing and running a successful legal research program. It is a great deal of hard work, but successful programs can form the basis of a fine working relationship between the library and the paralegals, and both will receive personal and professional satisfaction.

Thank you.

Helen Aikman Whitman

Legal assistants come from very diverse backgrounds. Most firms now have the requirement of a certificate, but the quality of legal assistant programs around the country is so uneven that even a certificate doesn't mean really anything in terms of what people really know. Furthermore, that standard is compromised a great deal when a client's son or daughter or a partner's son or daughter or niece or nephew needs a job. A lot of people, in spite of that standard, get hired without a certificate or any legal assistant training whatsoever. For this reason I think that generalized formal training programs for legal assistants, unless they are on a very small scale or simply review sources of information, are of very limited value.

For example, teaching a new legal assistant how to use the Bluebook is much more beneficial than teaching cite-checking per se.

I think that Connie's suggestion that you talk to the legal assistant supervisor, assuming that there is one, in formulating your training programs is a good one. I would suggest also that you speak with senior legal assistants. Connie painted a very bleak picture of what it's like in a paralegal program in a large law firm. Frankly, my experience is contrary to that. I know at Shaw, Pittman and other firms around town, we have many senior legal assistants. We have people at Shaw, Pittman who have been there for 15 years. We don't have a high turnover rate at all, people are very committed, they think of themselves as professionals, they have very good working relationships with the attorneys and they have very intimate involvement with the cases. I think if there are senior legal assistants, they are going to be intimately aware of the deficiencies in the training of the younger ones, because the younger ones will typically come to them with their problems.

One thing that is very different in training us than in training lawyers is that we are required to do a huge amount of factual research. It's dangerous for legal assistants to do much in the way of legal research actually and typically will have very limited assignments in legal research. But the factual research we are called on to do has no bounds. One week I may be asked to research the connection between hypoxic deliveries and cerebral palsy; the next week I may be asked to determine whether there is such a thing as a super drug store market. I mean that very literally. You get these very intensive yet diverse factual assignments.

What I think is of great value in training programs that I have encountered is for librarians to perform a mapping function. Washington is a real jungle of libraries. There are other law firms, universities, hospitals, trade associations — almost every trade association has a library of some form or other. When you have to find out if there is a super drug store market for antitrust purposes and you go to the business periodicals index and you find that there is a magazine called *Chain Drug Review*, and you can't find it anywhere in the library, and the Library of Congress only has it going back one year, then you can call some pharmaceutical association and they will have it going back fifteen years.

If we can receive a written document from librarians that identifies and gives addresses all of the libraries that are available in town, on the federal level, the state court, and the local libraries, I think that is a tremendous help.

The only other thing I wanted to comment on is on computer–assisted research. There's nobody in the world who can talk as fast as Mead Data Sales representatives. I have seen these people and they are marvelous. They know more than you can possibly imagine, but they talk so fast it's unbelievable how much they cover. I think that every training session given by an outside vendor should be supported by an in–house training session by the librarian stressing such practical matters as efficiency and cost.

Also, in the same sense that we are going to be going off–site to libraries doing factual research in the books more than attorneys, we will be doing more computer–assisted factual research than attorneys, and I think that you can give us a lot of guidance in that. To have a list of computer sources that are available is very helpful, particularly if we know what level of information we are going to get, so that we don't spend hours looking for the wrong things at great cost to clients.

One last thing about computer–assisted research. When we do research off–site in libraries or at government agencies such as the recorder of deeds office, or any of the numerous places that we are required to go off–site and do research, we find that each computer system in each institution is different. No two have the same instructions. They always have a little laminated sheet of paper that is beside the computer and it has fifteen steps on how to get on the system. But when we sit down at the terminal to read the instructions, twenty people are waiting in line behind us to use the computer. If our firm librarians can collect instructions for the computer systems around town at different institutions and even accompany a few legal assistants off–site once in a while for hands on training at, say, the Library of Congress, then you will be saving us much time and anxiety. It's really horrifying to go into a building we don't know, staffed by people we don't know, sign into a computer system we don't know and all the while to have people lined up behind us waiting and snapping their fingers and chewing gum. If we can sit down for 15 minutes before we leave our own offices and familiarize ourselves with the workings of the off–site computer system, it is very, very helpful.

Jim Hambleton

I hope that the panel discussions so far have provided some thoughts and ideas. We are going to break into smaller discussion groups with discussion leaders. I want people to go ahead and bring up some issues and then we will report back here in about 45 minutes for those discussion group reports. If everything goes according to plan, we should finish five to ten minutes early. We will have one representative of each of the five discussion groups summarize the highlights of that particular discussion group.

Gitelle Seer

It was clear from our group that one of the measures of how important this topic is was the fact that we barely scratched the surface. And, when our 45 minutes was up, everybody said "oh..." So, Jim said I should tell you we can all continue this conversation in the bar tonight after dinner.

Two issues came up. One was some ideas that people gave each other about effective orientation techniques, and the other one was a problem that I think we all share. Some of the ideas that came up I think we all agreed were very good. One of the issues we discussed was the fact that we overload people with information — lots of written stuff as part of orientation — because that's our business. And, we think the more we give them the more they will learn and the fewer questions they will ask us, and that is clearly not the case. What seems to be more effective is fewer pieces of paper or highlighting the really important things that they absolutely have to know.

I took that to heart because I give people at orientation a package like this, and then I wonder why they never open it; and it comes back to me all dust-covered when they leave. So, we are definitely going to try smaller packets and just focus on the things that new people really need to know.

One of the librarians said that she mails some of her orientation materials to her summer associates before they come to the firm. I thought that was another very good technique of connecting with them earlier on, plus giving them a little bit of time to read the materials before they come to the firm. This is the first summer she has done so — maybe next year she will report back on how well that works. But I thought that was an interesting technique to try as well.

It's pretty clear that the larger firms do more formal orientations. A couple of additional ideas on orientation techniques came up. One woman said that she uses a question-answer method as a way of getting people warmed up, because they have been listening to orientations that basically lecture to them and tell them what to do and tell them about the firm. One way to keep their interest and to make it interesting and get them interested is to ask questions about how they would solve a problem, what they know, and a little bit of a test just as kind of an opener.

Everybody agreed that you have to get to summer associates before they get their first assignment, whether or not that is the very first day. The second day is already too late. You have got to forge a bond with them and make them know what you know; and if they come to you as a resource, then it has got to be done right, early on.

We also talked about getting your staff involved in the library orientation, letting them talk to these summer associates about their areas of specialty. I have just started to do that and, considering how big my staff is and how long I have been around, it took me a long time to realize that that is very, very effective because attorneys connect with other people and start to understand a little bit more the scope of what we are capable of doing.

Those are some of the ideas. The problem issue that we discussed was working with paralegals. I think it struck a cord in everybody that we are not sure how to deal with them. We don't know what they don't know; they don't know what they don't know; we don't know what they need to know or how to teach them. I find that very difficult, as I said to my group. I have just dealt with it. I basically ignored it because I really don't know how to deal with 35 to 45 paralegals, all of whom have different experience, different expectations, different interests and even capabilities of learning what you have to teach them. So we batted around some ideas about what you could teach them, and we all realize that is a very touchy issue in each of our firms.

Debbie Pitts

I'm Debbie Pitts — I'm from Mead Data Central — L.A. Office — so I'm not a librarian, although I was a paralegal. We had a very interesting discussion of paralegals and it definitely is something that strikes lots of emotion into the hearts of a lot of librarians. When I was a paralegal, nobody knew what a paralegal was. The paralegal range is so wide, and you don't have that wide a range in librarians and attorneys. A lot of people — I know that a lot of the people in our group — felt that the paralegal who was speaking here was atypical.

Librarians are such a good resource, and they don't understand why paralegals weren't coming to them and asking for assistance. I think that people who don't realize what a resource all of you are, are really missing out on a tremendous opportunity to get their job done faster and better. I really agree with the librarians in our group who said that paralegals need to look at you in a different light.

Maybe it goes back to marketing. We talked about that also. In the resource category, you constantly have to market yourself to everybody, and, if you don't, paralegals won't know what a great resource they have in all of you.

We also talked about the basic training needs of everyone in the firm, and one of the ideas that came up was a basic lecture on civics. A lot of people just don't know basic civics. In addition, research skills, not only legal research skills but business and factual research skills, are not known by very many in the firm.

We had people talk about different techniques that they are using in teaching research. People are using different programs for the different levels in the firm, such as support staff, library staff, associates, paralegals and partners.

An excellent idea that came up was that all new support staff are to come to a once–a–month orientation on the library. That type of orientation is done by several different librarians. In fact, one librarian commented that because the orientation is conducted during the lunch hour, they pay their people for coming because it is so strongly encouraged.

Another idea that I thought was really interesting was to have an "introduction to law" class taught by an attorney on a monthly basis and covering questions such as what municipal bonds are or what a public offering is. A lot of people hear these phrases around the firm, and they don't know what they mean, so this is good public relations for attorneys.

In terms of how to get people to come to training, one of the most effective ways is to have food. That point kept coming out over and over again; food is something that people respond to. Training also helps in their job, their self–esteem, and it helps on the resume, too.

Cross–training is an important issue that also came out. As you mentioned, people do come to the library, and they talk to whomever is standing right there first, so cross–training is necessary. The issue of control came up also. You do have to use good judgment when cross–training.

A lot of good ideas came out, and I think our session was productive; we wished it could have been longer because a lot of good ideas were discussed.

Steven Lastres

I am Steve Lastres, librarian, Fulbright and Jaworski in New York. Our group focused on the type of legal research courses we teach in our law firms, and basically four out of the six librarians teach formal legal research courses. Some of them are incorporated into orientation. There was a question in terms of how to incorporate them. A couple of the larger firms incorporate their research training into the general orientation session to the firm, where all the different departments are represented. The librarians feel that this gives them more clout as part of the administrative staff.

Two of the other librarians said that they teach research courses independently of orientation so they get the full attention of all the summer associates. These librarians feel that this emphasizes that the librarian is special, and the librarian has a special hour or two hours to make a presentation, which was again generally done over food. The librarians felt that serving food eases summer associates; they are a little less nervous. You get to talk with them about personal situations, what they have been doing in law school and then, after the luncheon is done and everyone has eaten, everyone feels a little bit more comfortable and you can get down to business.

We all agreed that in our firms, it seems that the sessions are mandatory and are normally conducted during the first week or within the first couple of days after the summer associates arrive, before assignments are handed out, so you can get their full attention.

There was a concern from one of the librarians who will evaluate summer associates this year for the first time. Her firm doesn't have a recruiter, so she has been asked to evaluate the summer associates. She is concerned about what that means and what the ramifications are for them coming to the research session with an open mind, not having to be "tested" and evaluated. She questions what the evaluation factor is going to add to the research program and how it will affect the program.

A couple of other things that were mentioned were suggestions on incorporating LEXIS and Westlaw representatives. We see them, unfortunately, as just sales people, but we can use them more efficiently. One of the things we do in my firm is that we use vendor representatives to come in and give presentations on cost–effective research not mentioning their company affiliations, but just simply talking about topics such as how you can use CFR on–line to be more cost effective. Basically the librarian moderates, by interjecting comments such as, "Well, in my experience. . ." or "In particular types of research, it's more effective or more beneficial to use LEXIS or Westlaw."

One of the librarians felt strongly from hearing the partner speak today that the partner was advocating on–demand legal research. In other words, when the summer associate actually needs to know, that is the time to take the time out (15 to 20 minutes) and teach him a process like how to use the CFR. This librarian doesn't think the summer associates are getting full benefit from being in a lecture class and learning how to use the CFR and the List of Sections Affected. It is more appropriate for on–demand teaching. One of the things that she uses the orientation session on the library for is to market the library to state that information is power and that she has power because she has the key sources to information. This librarian tries to promote the library in that manner, and also she promotes the library as an ally, and that she is a friend and to come to her instead of a partner.

One of the other very good suggestions that came across was to teach summer associates reference skills so when they are getting an assignment from a partner, they can ask more questions that are pertinent to get more information from the partner. By narrowing down what type of response the partner is looking for from the summer associate, the summer associate won't come to the librarian and just say, "I need this" and then be evasive about what exactly they are looking for.

The other positive suggestion that came out of our discussion was that it was a good idea to get the summer assignments from the assigning partners prior to the summer associates coming to the firm, and to have a handle on what the summer associates are expected to know and to have the other reference librarians get involved. One of the larger firms said that, for example, summer associates consider the head librarian as the sole person in the library who can help them. When you incorporate your reference librarians, some of the larger firms who have specialized reference librarians find these librarians can come into the process, and the summer associates immediately realize there is more than one source in the library. This is especially important when you have 25 or 30 summer associates. It is very important for them to know the head librarian is not the only person who can be used.

Another very good idea which I thought was an excellent way to approach legal research is to use second–year associates. One librarian gets a couple of volunteers from second year who have just been through what these new associates are going to go through. Then she requests questions and answers from the second years that are instructive. Next the newer and older attorneys will go out for some beers after work and basically the assignments are distributed. The new associates are given two or three hours and told, "Here are the questions — see if you can get some answers." Then a couple of days later or a week later the new associates will get together with the second–year associates, who are their mentors and the second–year associates will just say "Well, this is good, you did this part of the research assignment well, but maybe you could have considered other options." That sounds to me like a very good idea because it does form a mentor/mentee relationship which, in private law firms, is usually not the case. You don't usually see that kind of bonding going on between the younger associates and the senior associates.

Basically, it was very important, at least the librarians thought it was very important, to make the summer associates understand that the library staff and the librarian are part of the overall administrative process and that we have a very important role within the firm. It was very important to make that clear right from the beginning.

New Speaker [name unavailable]

We became aware when the group first started talking there was a feeling that we would have liked to have had the opportunity to stay in the auditorium a little bit longer and do some question and answers with the people on the panel. There was a feeling of frustration that, especially where the paralegal was involved, there wasn't an opportunity to respond.

We did, I guess, vent our frustrations and focus a little bit on the paralegal, even though she wasn't present. It was very soon that we became aware of the fact that there is a lack of communication and a lack of understanding between what librarians do, what paralegals do, and how we need to help each other and how we need to work together.

It was a good learning experience for us to see how there can be an enormous gap in understanding, because the paralegal was suggesting things that are just so against what we are trying to instill in our paralegals and the people who work with them. Her suggestion that we give paralegals all the information they need to go knock on all the doors of all the libraries in town would mean that no librarian would ever talk to us again.

The paralegal seems to have missed the point that there is a need to have some kind of centralized control so that people aren't asking the same questions over and over again, buying the same books over and over again, hitting the same resources over and over again, and calling around to find out what resources are available in different locations when we are sitting there with a union list right behind our chair. This in fact is our job.

Information is our business, and we need to let the paralegals know that we would love to help them with this, but the way for us to help them is to encourage them to understand when it is appropriate to come to us. So we spent a lot of time focusing on the paralegal.

We then took some time to go into response to what Richard had been talking about — the training of lawyers and new associates, and there was some understanding that Richard's point is well taken, that the fact is that they do arrive not well trained, but that the law schools really do need to continue to focus on teaching legal bibliography and legal research. We can do our part but, we can only fill in the gaps. There is a need to realize that we only see the cream of the crop, a small percentage of those students who graduate from law school. Many graduates go on to firms that don't have librarians that can fill in this research gap or to be sole practitioners or to other kinds of experiences where there is no one to teach them. We can do our part, and we will do the best we can, but law schools really need to continue to focus on teaching legal bibliography and legal research.

There was also a feeling that law schools are doing better in this — they are focusing more on it, realizing that they need to continue to teach legal bibliography and legal research; and that we, of course, continue to need to fill in the gaps. We need to ascertain where new associates research skills are and what their training has been. When the new associates arrive at the firm and we see they have the basics, then we can concentrate more on research in the subject areas of their specialties.

When our session was breaking up, someone stopped me in the hall and said, "We really didn't have a chance to concentrate that much on talking about what our individual programs were in our individual firms, and I would really have liked to have heard that." I'm suggesting we all take the opportunity to continue sharing that information with each other over dinner and the cocktail hour. I think that is enormously valuable and that we can all come away learning from each other.

New Speaker [name unavailable]

I'm just going to highlight the things that were not already discussed. Two of our people are responsible for a MCLE in their firms. I thought that was a very interesting point and something that many might want to think about.

It was generally acknowledged, I think, that everybody had some sort of program for secretaries; and everybody seemed to agree that secretaries were one of the groups that were easiest to provide a program for because their needs were very clear, and apparently, they are very, very responsive. So there was a lot of agreement on secretaries. I think everything has been said already about paralegals.

People have done a variety of things. Some people are doing formal 12-week programs and find that they have been very well received. There is a problem with the question of time — how much time this takes away from their other activities.

There was a little discussion about how you might cover for lost time. You can hire consultants to come in and teach, and I broached the question of why can't you present yourself to the firm as the consultant for whom you were going to contract out. You will provide this extra service to the firm for X dollars and when they reject that, then you hit them with some kind of extra staff to do the routine work while you are off doing the training. Maybe it will work — maybe it won't.

This is something for Mead to note. Two people said that an idea came out of Graylyn that they have implemented — exchanging librarians between law firms and law schools. I thought that that's something positive that Mead would want to know about — that these programs do cause some action, and on my little learning model, what you are trying to do is change behavior when you are doing training, and that certainly illustrates changing behavior.

Somebody mentioned in reference to Rich's comments about training partners that he had found in his firm that there was a real need to train partners when partners went into a new line of practice, such as international trade. This is something that the firm had not done before, so all of a sudden they have a new department in a new practice area. In some cases, there is a partner in charge of a new department and that partner does not know the research sources. I don't know why this would happen, but it does. You sometimes have a labor attorney suddenly in charge of the tax department. That person needs a very quick tutorial in the research resources of that new area.

Jim Hambleton

I, too, was interested in what the legal assistant had to say. Last year I was program chair of the Dallas Association of Law Librarians. My theme for the year was "expanding our professional horizons, other organizations and institutions." As part of that ongoing program, I invited the presidents of the different associations in the local area to come and talk to our group. I had the President of the Legal Administrators and I also had the President of the Dallas Association of Legal Assistants come address us. The legal assistant's presentation was very interesting because as she got into it, she talked about the kinds of things that legal assistants do, such as LEXIS and Westlaw searches, and she was very surprised to find out that librarians do those searches, too. Through the course of her discussion it became clearer and clearer that the paralegal was infuriating the law librarians in the audience in that she had no concept at all of what librarians do in a law firm, and here she was, the President of the Dallas Association of Legal Assistants.

A lot of librarians were very upset with me for having the paralegal present a program, and they came up to me afterwards saying, "Why did you have her? She clearly has no idea what we do." I said, "Yes, librarians talk to each other, but look at your firm and look at the power legal assistants have." Legal assistants tend to be seen much more on the part of law firm administration as part of the legal team, they have much higher visibility. In a lot of firms, they are treated much better than law firm librarians. They were the first non–lawyers invited to join the American Bar Association. Their national organization complained because "L.A. Law" didn't have a legal assistant, and they actually had a legal assistant in one of the shows because of that. They are a much more powerful and effective lobby group. As a group then, law librarians might have something to learn from paralegals, and it is in our best interest to forge closer ties with legal assistants.

Closing Conference Summation

Bob Berring

There is something especially daunting about rising to take the place as final speaker at the conference. We have gone through three days of frenetic and productive activity, three days of listening, talking and learning. But I am filled with energy and inspirations by what has happened at this conference. It is a fitting successor to the Graylyn conferences that have been so successful in bringing together people from academic law libraries to talk about the problems of teaching legal research. The idea of bringing together law firm librarians, the people who are doing so much of the real on–the–job training on the battlefield of legal research, is timely and much needed. Before I go to the heart of my remarks, I want to take the time to thank the people who have put this conference together. It is thus with genuine admiration that I recognize how well planned and coordinated this event has been. I want to take a moment to thank all of the people whose names appear in the tiny–sized print at the beginning of your program. The Conference Council, Marie Wallace, Victoria Trotta, Jim Hambleton, Barbara Geier, Gitelle Seer and Suzanne Zumbro did a marvelous job in pulling together this program.

Mead Data Central brought us together and provided us with this beautiful forum for the meeting to happen; they have been willing to let us talk to each other and learn from each other, without imposing their views or advertising upon us. Mead Data Central has been content to stay in the background, allowing the very positive energy that has developed here to proceed on its own. I salute them for their generosity in providing us with a forum, and their marvelous restraint in staying in the background.

This makes me think about the past three days and the program itself. We had a very challenging agenda set before us, and thinking back over the past seventy–two hours it's almost hard to believe that we've only been here three days.

ELECTRONIC MEDIA AND THE TRANSFORMATION OF LAW

Ethan Katsh, the author of *The Electronic Media and the Transformation of Law*, set forth some of the most important ideas of the last ten years. He gave us a broad theme that we can all draw from and that tied the entire program together. In talking about how information and its environment is changing, and how people will perceive information in a new and different way, he gave us excellent examples of the fact that we don't step back often enough to consider the context in which we work. We are probably in the middle of what historians will view as an information revolution, and Professor Katsh has allowed us to see a bit of that revolution. Applying some information theory to law is a great beginning for opening up our minds.

PRESENTATION SKILLS

Into that opening stepped Ben Swett, who came from the UCLA Comedy College to talk to us about the use of humor in presentations. Now I had been told that Ben was one half of a comedy team, and since only one of them showed up I thought we might receive only one half of a presentation. But in fact Ben did a terrific job, he broke down humor into comprehensive categories and showed us through his "how to be a geek" approach that we can turn our own weaknesses into strengths. Lawyers are aggressive animals who frequently flourish in a jungle of verbal aggression, and therefore the use of humor would be especially helpful to all of us. Law professors and partners all take themselves too seriously and sometimes need to be lightened up with some humor.

HOW TO LECTURE EFFECTIVELY

The next presentation was that of Ann Bateson. Ms. Bateson should have come at the end of the program. Not so much because intellectually she belonged there, but because she made it so hard for the rest of us. Ms. Bateson told us how one lectures well, how one reaches an audience and how one communicates ideas. That created a problem for all of us. She did such a good job of setting out how one is supposed to communicate information that every speaker was thinking, "How am I ever going to live up to her standards?" But it was worth it. I am a compulsive note taker and I ended up with a million notes, providing some fantastic overviews. The program dared to be great. It put the big stuff at the beginning, how to think about information, how to communicate humor and how to get your audience involved, then it set about looking at the information from different angles.

BRIDGING THE GAP — LAW SCHOOL TO LAW FIRM

Next David Feldman told us about his different identities. He presented his view of the world from several perspectives: as a law student, as a video producer, as a summer associate and as a lawyer. He also informed everybody that some people take my Advanced Legal Research class because they think it is a "gimme" — I don't think David realizes that you can change people's grades retroactively! But he gave us all an enormous amount of insight. Maybe the most stunning single fact that I learned at the conference came from David when he pointed out that the average law student of today was fourteen years old when MTV first appeared. I think that's a wonderful way to think of the audience that we have to reach. We are attempting to communicate legal research skills to folks who grew up watching Michael Jackson videos. Understanding that is going to be crucial.

RESEARCH INSTRUCTION FOR PARTNERS, ASSOCIATES AND SUMMER ASSOCIATES

Richard Leiter brought us back with a very careful working through of the elements of teaching legal research. Mr. Leiter carefully analyzed who we were teaching, how we were teaching and why we were teaching. He provided us with a lattice work of patterns for organizing our thinking and for considering our own approach. It was a wonderful kickoff to the first afternoon session.

Connie Dickson talked to us about how to train support staff. She painted what I thought was a realistic picture of what life is like in some large law firms. She set out the challenges that the firm librarian must meet in training and interacting with support staff personnel. It was a useful set of insights.

Ellen Callinan then joined the program. Ms. Callinan has written one of those articles which I used to call seminal. But some years ago one of my students at Berkeley criticized me, saying that I should alternate my use of the word seminal with that of the word, ovarian. Therefore, I will say that Ms. Callinan has written an ovarian article on teaching in a law firm setting. Her recent piece in *Law Library Journal* is one that we all will be referring back to for years. No matter if you approve of her approach or disapprove, her article will be the first piece to cite because she has defined a whole new range of discussion. And in that way she exemplified what was happening in this program. We are talking about an entirely new area, one that is crucially important and yet which is still being defined, "the teaching of research skills in the law firm environment." She also told us to start small and to build up. It was an inspiring and realistic presentation.

We had some reactors who commented on the speeches. Jeff Pash, a partner at Covington and Burling, stayed on the bottom line, telling us in practical and realistic ways what a law firm expects. Mr. Pash made me feel old, since he gave the insights of a "seasoned" researcher and I discovered that he sat in on my legal research lectures at Harvard. But I forgive him.

Helen Aikman Whitman woke us all up with her view of what librarians ought to be doing and ought to be teaching from the perspective of a paralegal. If the true job of the middle of the afternoon speaker is to electrify, she belongs on the all-star team. Many people wanted to react to her remarks and wanted to explain to her how she misperceived the librarian's role. Her talk fired us up, and that is just what it should have done.

One thing I began to notice at this point, as I looked over my notes, was how many different constituencies we were bringing together in this meeting. I became aware of how many different viewpoints were banging into each other and the energy that was being generated by the collision. Yet this was only the beginning, because the program was going to pull in more people with different views from an even greater array of places. We all went to breakout groups then, for small group discussions. The energy produced by the lectures fed into those groups, and when the person chosen by each group came to summarize their group's discussion for the general audience the heart of it was that each group had more to say when time ran out. Even at the end of a long day people had more ideas to share. We weren't losing energy, we were building up energy as we went along. Usually at the end of the day people are dead, but this room was filled with people who were fired up. It was genuinely exciting.

OPTIONS FOR TEACHING RESEARCH

What happened on Saturday? Well, Jean O'Grady described the successful program that she runs at Shea and Gould, setting out an excellent model for how to do it well. One of the most frequently belittled speeches is the "how I do it good" type of speech, but in this area, where we are all feeling our way, we need to hear about successful models and how they have been pulled off. It goes without saying that Jean was also very funny.

Then Timm Whitney talked about the program at Morgan, Lewis and Bockius, a program that is just beginning. It was an interesting presentation, all the more so because Mr. Whitney represented yet another group. He was a personnel coordinator for his firm, representing another profession involved in the training of lawyers. He not only brought news of his firms's program but also insight from an entirely different group. I sat next to Mr. Whitney at dinner and he talked about the National Association for Law Placement and I began to see how this other group blended into the entire picture.

Stephanie Heacox then provided us with a presentation that I genuinely enjoyed. Ms. Heacox discussed her regiment for training people on how to use online databases. She told us how to make creative use of user fear and she gave us some terrific tricks of the trade on how to get lawyers to pay attention and not to waste time when conducting LEXIS and Westlaw searches. She kept us enlightened and entertained. A terrific presentation, I thought.

Karen Brunner talked to us about interactive video and how it can be used in skills training. I'd never seen an interactive video program presented before, so it was extremely interesting for me to see one that was up and running and successful. It showed the fantastic possibilities of the creative use of technology.

Ellen Miller of Harvard Law School then joined us. Ms. Miller represented yet another constituency. Here is someone who went out on her own and created an entire audiovisual department at that great fortress, Harvard Law School, a place that is famous for resisting any change and which says it doesn't care about research and wouldn't care even if it was supposed to. Yet Ms. Miller has created the most dynamic audiovisual operation in the country. She went out and made her own show and she is now the leader in a whole new field. Ms. Miller is another pioneer in the program, and one who is willing to share her insights on how to make a good video. She showed us what works and what doesn't and gave practical tips as well as theory. This was the hallmark of the program. Not only did you learn about things, you learned how to really do things.

JOINT VENTURE: LAW SCHOOLS AND LAW FIRMS

At that point, the program did one of the most amazingly courageous things I've ever seen. After a Saturday afternoon off, the organizers scheduled a Saturday evening program. Fortunately they were able to go out and bring in some heavy artillery for speakers who kept us awake and on the edge of our seats through the three hours. Warren Rosmarin of the University of Miami Law School talked about what an aggressive law school program can accomplish and how to get there. Warren is another pioneer, someone to create new models, use other people's models, twist them all together, bang them on the side and come out with something new and positive. He sounded the note of cooperating with law firms and building bridges between academic and law firm librarians. It was full of ideas as well as insight. And Warren was, as ever, very, very funny.

Allan Holoch of Ohio State followed up with a discussion of what Ohio State is doing with law firms in Columbus. We heard about creative ideas, how to stretch resources, how to get the law firm librarians into the law firm. Naturally that creative stat of Ohio would be the home of the Football Hall of Fame, and of course, my beloved birthplace. And it is also the home of Dayton, Ohio. Let's face it, if you drop a marble onto a map of the United States it's always going to roll to Dayton.

Both Warren and Allan gave us pictures of creative energy between law firms and law schools, how the sum can be greater than the parts and how resources can be maximized.

Nora Skrukrud from the Crosby, Heafey law firm in Oakland, California then told us about what her firm is doing. She talked about the experiences that have been gathered from law firms in Northern California and how some of the innovations that are going on in her firm and others in the Bay Area in working with the law schools in the area have produced excellent results. Nora and I have been on a series of programs together now, and I still manage to learn from her every time.

Then Steve Margeton of American University Law School, gave us a theoretical overview of the situation and how we got here. He gave us the structure with which to fit everything we had heard up to that point. We ended Saturday still buzzing, still talking in the hallway, still full of ideas. The great risk had worked.

PROFESSIONAL DEVELOPMENT PROGRAMS

Then this morning, the last day, we say the perfect way to close this conference. Today we had the viewpoint from consultants, people who will come into your law firm and tell you what the broad range of your needs are. In this way we went from the broad to the specific, how you figure out exactly what your firm needs. We had Carolyn Wehmann, a consultant, who can tell you how to figure out what you needs are. Ms. Wehmann is another pioneer. Here is a person who started her own company, who told us how she did it and how she can help you create your own program. She represents yet another constituency, the professional education consultant, but she framed things in terms that we could understand and gave us useful hints on how to decide whether we even need a consultant. She was refreshingly honest and entertaining.

Kathy Morria Mejia told us how she worked in one particular law firm environment. It was a terrific story. She described how she was hired by the law firm who had rejected her idea to hire a person like her. It was a wonderful reflection of the way law firms work but also the way persistence pays off.

Finally we had Richard Lee, another pioneer, in fact this time someone who created a whole field. Dick Lee is the king of in-firm training programs, someone who's been in academia, in practice and now concentrates on training. They are starting their own national association, so a few years from now, we can tell him that we saw him at the ground floor. Mr. Lee gave us an overview of what is going on, presenting the picture at the macro partner level, ending the program with the kind of assessment that we would love to hear given to the partners in our law firms and the senior professors at our law school.

SUMMATION

Maybe I can give you a few ideas to walk out of here thinking about. Perhaps I can draw from that enormous energy shown in this conference and provide you with a frame on which to hang some of the things that have happened and some of the wonderful ideas the speakers have laid out before me. Let me give you some things you can reject, things you can recast in your own light, and things you can remember. I want to share with you what I think are four great truths.

Truth number one: legal research is important. It has value. This is a truth I think most of us have a handle on, obviously you are enthused and you do care. I've seen that, you are here and you have taken time out of your busy work schedules.

But when you bang your head against the wall of indifference in your organization, there is always going to be that nagging doubt, is legal research important? Yes it is. Can it be taught? It absolutely can be taught. Does it have to be taught? It absolutely, positively has to be taught.

Why do I say that? I say that because we heard about competing interests. You are going to hear more about them. I hear about them in the law schools. You hear about them in your law firms and your agencies or wherever you work. You hear about them in the large database corporation events.

It is always going to be a matter of competing resources. Everybody is willing to genuflect to legal research. It has got to be the apple pie/motherhood issue of legal practice. We have all heard partners, administrators and deans say, "Yes, research is important, by golly, and I rank it right up there with writing. Nobody knows how to write anymore and they don't know how to research." Or perhaps they say, "Look at these young, fuzzy–faced computer jockey associates, we pay them twice as much as I made when I started and they wouldn't know Shepard's if it bit them." Yet, our complainers are not willing to do anything about it.

At the Graylyn conference this past fall, I received a wonderful lead–in from Professor Arthur Miller who was also one of the keynote speakers. He gave a fantastic description of education at the Harvard Law School. And what do they do at Harvard Law School? Professor Miller started out by saying how important, how crucial legal research was, how glad he was to be there. He said, "What do we in legal education do well?" and I remember it was a great analogy, he said, "We teach the students to peel the onion, that's what we do, the onion of analysis, peel off the skin, layer by layer." I always wondered what they were doing to me in the first year. Now I found out. They were peeling my onions.

And then he said, "What do we not do well? Well we don't teach legal research very well, but I'm sure you folks will figure that out." I don't mean to be unfair to Professor Miller. He is typical. Like other faculty, like many lawyers, he will genuflect to legal research training but will not commit resources to it. We have seen that. Now that there is a whole new world of professional training and professional development, there is going to be even more competition for resources. In-house training is hot. But that puts us back into competition. Do you train them to do depositions? Do you train them in trial practice? Do you train them in appellate practice? Do you train them in legal research? You must be a believer that it can be done and it is important.

Truth number two: We are the good humans. I say this because in many ways we represent the interests of the associates, the students or the staff even if they don't recognize it themselves. Rich Leiter did a great job of sketching out the reasons why we teach legal research; he analyzed the motivation. Part of it he told us is sanity. We teach legal research skills to our students, associates or support staff to stay sane.

To keep from being driven crazy by responding to the same questions seventy-two times is a powerful motivation. You get sensory overload from being hit upon by the thirteenth associate that day who is in the midst of the most important crisis that she will ever be in during her entire life, until she gets that particular question answered right now.

You have to save yourself from that, but we are also there to help. We are there to teach them a skill, to make them invest time now and save time later. It's almost a parental model. I hate to use that analogy, but it almost is. We have to invest capital now. Dick Lee talked about that, but the young lawyers often don't see that, and so many times the organizations in which they operate don't see it.

By helping them learn these skills well in the beginning, not only will they benefit, but we also will keep our sanity.

We are one of the few groups who are there to help them learn a skill and send them on their way. We should never lose sight of the fact we are virtuous. If they succeed, we succeed. We are not looking at them through gimlet eyes of calculation. We really want them to succeed. Good legal research training meets John Rawl's test, it makes everybody better off.

What is truth number three? Truth number three is something that has really surfaced at this conference: It's a New World.

What do I mean by that? We are in the middle of seeing a change in the way people practice law, and the way legal education is carried out. This change is creating a whole series of challenges and opportunities. There are risky paths here, but taking risks often provides opportunities.

Let's look at the various levels here. Who is our audience? Who are we trying to teach? We are trying to teach partners, senior associates, junior associates, new associates, support staff, library personnel and paralegals.

We have to recognize that there is a generational change that is going on in the use of information. This is where I become the other half of the Ethan Katsh sandwich. Because I think that the average person's perception of information is changing in a way that is very difficult for us to understand.

As most of you know, I am incredibly nearsighted. I've been that way since birth. Although I wear the best contact lenses known to human kind, my correction is still far from normal. When I was a child, the doctor told my parents that I shouldn't read more than one book a week. So, what did I do? I became a guerrilla reader. There used to be a book mobile where I lived and I would pay other kids to get me books.

I used to hide books. I had books hidden under tree stumps, I hid books under the dock, which actually is a long story in itself. Reading became my obsession. I read as much as I could get my hands on, displaying that perverse devotion that children so delightfully have of doing exactly what is wrong for them.

So I've grown up. I collect books. I surround myself with books. My default activity is reading. If I'm not doing anything else, I'm reading. So if there is ever a person who appreciates and loves books, it is me.

It is very difficult for us to understand this. It is a generational change, and such changes are very difficult for anybody who is older to understand. The students I see in my classes, graduates and undergraduates, are the video generation. The get their information on video and they are growing up naturally attuned to computers. Their default activity is playing Nintendo or using a computer.

I set up a workstation in my house last semester while I was on sabbatical. With some help, I set the computer up, I got a modem, I souped up the computer and I was ready. The first day I sat down to work, I was going to carefully work through my new software programs and read all the directions. I turned on the screen and the first thing I saw was a file named "Simon." Simon is my older son who at the time was only five and one-half years old.

They were using Macs in his preschool and he knew how to go in, open a file and type his own name. There wasn't anything in it, but I thought, "My God, what is he going to be like when he is in college? What is he going to be like if he is a law student?"

The folks produced by this change are just going to be different and they will use information in a different way, and that's very, very hard for us to see and almost impossible for some of our decision makers to understand. That's one of the reasons why we have to know what we are doing is important and that we are the forces of good, because we have to translate some of those needs. And being the translator is hard work.

The people who have the new set of needs can't even see what they are asking for themselves, because they only know their own model. The older generation can't really understand it either. We only know the model of research that we have for ourselves.

There is another big siege going on and all of you are a part of it and I have learned a good bit about it since I have been here. That change is the way in which law is practiced.

I participated in a seminar last year at Berkeley because I am working on a piece about the concept of professionalism using librarians and lawyers as two contrast groups. One thing quickly became obvious — there are a lot of people working on lawyers, including sociologists and anthropologists. They are studying the large firm environment, and I heard a woman talk about her preliminary research. She had surveyed senior partners, older partners, in a variety of large law firms, and she reported that, uniformly, they are unhappy. Uniformly, they feel the world has changed, it is not like it was in "my" time. They feel that law has become a cutthroat business, it is all bottom line, it is all cash flow.

At the Graylyn Conference sponsored by Mead Data Central this fall, I heard a talk which I've quoted a lot since. A fellow named Diamond, who is the managing partner for Skadden Arps in Los Angeles, told us, "I am here because legal research is important, because you are part of overhead and that is all we have left. If we are going to squeeze out any more profit, it's got to come from overhead. Since we have got our associates cranked up to 2200–2400 billable hours a year, there is just no more you can get out of them."

He said, "Why, we already have somebody who will buy their clothes. We have people who will go out and shop for them and this year we hired a service which will go to the store to get groceries for them and put the food in their refrigerator. We just don't see where else we can go. Savings will have to come from overhead."

The person standing next to me turned to me and said, "I wonder if they would consider surrogate families?" You know, like someone could go out and get married for you and drop by once a week and say, "Well, the kids are doing great. The toilet is backed up, but the house is fine."

Mr. Diamond also told us that they have done the same thing with partners. Everybody is at full tilt bogie, they just can't get much more juice out of the orange at this point. They have to go after overhead.

That's the environment we are living in. Of course not everybody is there yet, it starts with the largest firms, but it is trickling down. So it's a different environment when we talk about things like training resources, it is a very different world that we are living in.

What is the fourth truth? The fourth truth is power. We live in a bottom–line universe and we need to understand and use power if we are to survive.

That means that librarians, whether they are in academic situations or whether they are in law firm situations, have to understand how to deal with power and how to assert themselves.

I see this cutting across librarianship on every front. Every part of librarianship, I think, is at the edge of both risk and opportunity right now, and law firm librarians are the cutting edge of that development.

Why is that? It is because in the firm environment, there is a large cash flow. The stakes of the game mean that the law firm library is running ahead of things. If you can justify expenses, you can often carry them out. Legal information is the richest information source out there. I think it is richer than medicine because of the competition in the private sector.

The richness makes power crucial, because power is linked to money. Think of my four truths together. It is important to do research training well. We are the good guys in all of this. We understand the sea of change that is going on. We have students who use their information differently and yet live in a universe with partners who don't.

Even if you could educate that partner or that senior associate to use the database because it is efficient, it's not going to be his or her default activity. This is going to be the way they view the universe, and it is the way people coming from college view it right now.

What do we do with my four great truths? We integrate them and bring them to bear on our own special problem, the problem of how we teach legal research skills in the law firm environment.

Are the law schools going to do it? You heard a great summary of problems the law schools are going to have. I don't have to reprise what Steve Margeton told you or what Warren Rosmarin confronted you with.

I just don't think you could have realistic expectations that training is going to happen the first year for the economic reasons that were pointed out. The professors are not going to give up the time.

Oh, they will genuflect to the importance of the enterprise, but they will not give up the time. These courses are being taught by the wrong people.

Remember what Steve Margeton told us about talking to the person who runs his law school's first-year research and writing program? It was a separate enterprise. If the library is not involved, I guarantee you that research is not a part of it. It is not even the land of the one-eyed leading the blind. It's the land of the half-eyed leading the blind, and no legitimate learning is going to happen. It would cost too much money and too much investment of time.

At Berkeley, the law school faculty had a retreat over the holidays at the end of the year. We talked about the future of our curriculum, and I made a pitch for increasing the seriousness and scope of skills training and they just said, "Not our stuff." One could give a whole lecture about the problems of a professional school that desperately wants to be academic. They have to be holier-than-thou on a research campus. At the law schools that aspire to rational status, it will be very hard to build really effective research training programs. It can happen, but it needs luck, sweat and the fire of a zealot. Second and third year advanced legal research courses hold out hope. That's what I've turned to as a solution, but it's only a partial solution because of some of the reasons that we have pointed out here.

Even though I've got 45 contact hours, I can't possibly speak intelligently to my students about specific areas. I can't make them do some of the hard stuff. I can make them understand how to use sets, and I can teach them the large patterns. I can try to teach them how to understand how information fits together so they can analyze any tool.

We took over the first-year program this year. Kathleen Vanden Heuvel and I teach the Advanced Legal Research course and this year for a set of special reasons, we took over the research part of the first–year writing and research course. We used the same number of hours (five) in the first–year program as the old program. We had five lecture hours, which is what they had always had.

I told the students, "Number one, you are not learning legal research in these five yours. Don't fool yourself. We are teaching you survival skills." We talked about how to use the library, we talked about primary sources, and you know what we gave them for assignments? We decided that the "search and destroy" research problem method, the kind where students look for specific cases, was ridiculous. It's busy work for them, a pain for us and nothing gets learned

Why make them do it in the first place? Naturally, we showed them where things were located in the library. But we wanted to do more than show them the books, we wanted them to understand case reporters. To accomplish this we had them take a case and look at it in U.S. Supreme Court Reports, the Supreme Court Reporter and Lawyer's Edition and write a book review. We asked them what was different about these three printings, why do three exist, is there different information in each, compare the indexing system, etc. We asked them to approach it as if they were normal human beings, not law students. They had some very interesting insights. We also made them look up, read and interpret a statute and we made them use citators.

One of the speakers here talked about the fact that research courses don't make people read. That's one of the luxuries of advanced legal research. We give them open–ended questions. They ended up all over the library. They picked their own case, picked their own jurisdiction and followed their own course. I never ask a question in advanced legal research that I already know the answer to. We almost always ask questions that have intrigued us, and that way, they don't all go to one place, and they have to go read the stuff.

Yet despite the positive efforts being made at law schools, it seems clear to me that law schools will not do the job if they don't have the will or way. So, does that mean law firms are going to be the answer? Maybe so; in any case law firm librarians can play a very special and useful role. You can work with law schools, and I think some of the interaction that has taken place here is some of the most exciting talk that I have heard in years. It's a powerful thought that firm librarians can come to the law school and make a contribution and that law school folks, despite limited resources, can somehow penetrate into the firm community. That's a really helpful and useful bond, and I think that's a bond that we absolutely have to exploit.

You heard last night in the question period that I have had a couple of students this year who during their job interview asked to see the law firm's library. One reason why this happened is because I asked a whole string of very fired up, competent people like Nora Skrukrud, to come speak to my class. My students see where power and potential lie. I always ask a law firm librarian to come and speak to my Advanced Legal Research class, and one of the things the librarians always makes clear is the level of resources available.

One of the other things that always comes across to students is one of the great truths, that we are the good guys. When you get a crazed assignment from this seemingly insane partner, you can go to the librarian and say, "I've got this crazed assignment from this seemingly insane partner." And the librarian can tell you, "Actually, that partner is not seemingly insane, he is insane. This happens all the time; don't worry, that's Mr. Gobongo. You'll only rotate there two weeks, just stay low. He brings in a lot of business; we've got to live with him."

The students discover that you are a clearinghouse, you are a socialization place, and you are one of the nonthreatening places in the firm, because every other associate, no matter how much they work with them, are ultimately competing with them.

And senior associates are competing and even partners are now competing. Someone asked a great question at the end of this morning's session when they asked if partners ever evaluate partners. All of the friends who went to law school with me and who are now partners sound like they evaluate each other constantly. They evaluate each other about points and how much money they take home. So there is enormous competition, eyeballing and side glances. But the firm librarian can actually help. You're like the Red Cross in a battle zone.

Now where do we fit in the training process? That's a question that every law firm person has to answer for him or herself. The type of highly articulated program that Dick Lee described to us this morning is not a program I think that most librarians can take over, or would want to run. Perhaps some do, but that is a career move.

Most of the "outside" folks who came to Westfields, folks who aren't librarians but who perform some function that is related to librarians, have recognized there is a certain bundle of expertise that we have, things that we do that are special and can't be done any other way.

I think that is something we have to treasure and to hold on to for these reasons. We understand how to manage information. It is our role, and we can continue to establish our value with this set of skills. I don't want to give that up, but I think that legal research training is so important that we have to fight for our share of the pie.

I'm saying "our" because the same thing is true in the academic environment. Academic law librarians have to justify themselves, they have to fight to be in that program. You have to fight to be so obvious and so involved, that when someone asks a person like Dick Lee, what does the legal research part of your program look like? He's going to know it cold. His librarian is going to be banging on his head about it all the time.

You have to show the associates that you are cost effective. Now we saw all kinds of great ways to do this. Jean O'Grady talked about a program she has already designed. Timm Whitney talked about what they are doing.

You might employ various types of technology, you can use on-line, you can use video; computer-assisted instruction might even play a role. Whatever the blend is in your firm, you have to be the pioneer. Just ask people here who are pioneers. In a way you are all pioneers, because when you go back to your firm, you have to carve out a slot for yourself. You have to fight for your turf. Everyone here is involved in a creative enterprise. It's new — we're making it up as we go along.

THREE RULES FOR INFORMATION SPECIALISTS

I guess that leads me to the three rules or three suggestions that I will leave you with about the future.

Number one: Identify your allies. One of our most basic allies is each other, and that is probably the most healthy thing I heard here. The networking between academics and private sector people has to be strong. I was in AALL at the point when the association almost split. The law firm folks almost split off. They had every possible good reason. Academic types had dominated power for way too long and there is no doubt about that. But the Association held, and in holding together we gained power. We have so much to gain from each other, so much to learn from each other. This conference has shown repeated examples of how we can work together.

We can use our combined energy to bring the message to the right people that legal research is important. We are together in this. Since we have a reference desk and you have a reference desk, we are going to see the same faces. The associate that you see in the firm is going to come back to us with her research assignments, then we'll send her back to you.

Are there other allies? I think there are. You know the bottom line is money and power, and the power in the firm is going to be with the lawyers. There is just no doubt about that. Someone said to me just now at the coffee break, "In our firm when we hit times of austerity and we have to cut, what do we cut? Staff. We don't cut the big ticket items, the lawyers, and that is because the lawyers understand what they do." Well there is no "them" and "us" in librarianship, and I think there should be an alliance struck with the professional development people. There should be alliances struck with the in-house training people. We should work as a team

The second tip: We have to plot. That is what this conference should be viewed as, a strategy session.

Who can we plot with? I think there is a set of allies we ought to be identifying, and that is the vendors.

This conference showed how Mead Data Central has a legitimate interest in helping. For a long time we have been treating the vendors with ten-foot poles, and there is always going to be some of that. Obviously, they want to sell us their stuff. They are bottom line, too. They have got their own internal corporate structure. We know that. However, they have got shared interests with us and those shared interests involve the intelligent use of their materials. They have gotten better about not shilling their products constantly. It's not in their best interest to do so. They are beginning to recognize that we are a sophisticated audience. And we are a group that needs help. We have to turn to our vendors as an ally just like the people within our firm, the people within our profession. We should turn to our vendors in structuring intelligent training packages. They have resources, expertise and good people. We have to work with them.

You can go to the vendors and say we need X. Get help. Use their creativity. You have to always be careful, but they are a potential ally that can be used. Plot with them, so that you can go in and say, "I've gotten together with the professional development people at my firm, and here's the package that I have put together." I would be happy as an academic to be part of that kind of package.

Number three? Dare to do it. There are different kinds of risk. There is stupid risk, and there is planned risk. The stupid risks are things that adolescents do. Planned risk is where you see an opportunity and you move towards it. Just as I said before, it is an incredible time of transition in librarianship, a time when the role of libraries could become more powerful or less powerful, it could become proactive or it can be reactive and we can become a vestigial profession. That's the risk we run.

Firm librarians have a great opportunity right now, and that is to seize a role in this training process. Everybody admits there is a problem with the research training skills of new associates. There is an open nerve right now because there is cognitive dissonance between what new lawyers are being paid to do and what they are capable of doing.

Someone is going to solve that problem. Someone is going to step in. It could be any of a number of solutions. It could be something research attorneys will develop, it could be something that professional continuing legal education programs will develop. A whole new profession might rise up. But it could be housed in a bond between the academics and the private library sector, and I think we have to dare to take that risk. I know that many of you are already overworked and overburdened, but this is a way to make yourself more important in your organization. This change is coming and someone is going to ride this change into power.

What would I do? What I would do is look for my allies, that is going to be different whatever firm situation you are in, but you must identify them and that includes the vendors.

I am going to plot with those people to try to come up with the best possible plan. Now before I go the last stage, remember our four truths. That's why I put them at the beginning. Sometimes when I speak to groups, they say this whole business sounds too conspiratorial. Folks tell me that I have really gotten lost in the commando thing. What do you mean plot, find allies? But remember our truths, we are the forces of good. We really are. Virtuous people have to be just as tough and nasty as bad people; otherwise, the bad people win.

If you don't want to be involved in this, then build your empire elsewhere. But I assume if you came here, you are interested. And if you are interested, there is risk here. This is an incredible opportunity. Ten years from now, what I really would love to do is see Mead Data Central sponsor a "ten years after" conference. We would all come back and I hope we can legitimately say, "They have better research skills. The problem is not solved, but we have made some real progress and these days, when we talk about training and legal research and the law schools and the law firm, it's the librarians who were the major players, because we had the guts to take the challenge on and the vision to solve it." Thanks.

Appendix

Presentation Skills Module Handbook

Westfields Conference on Teaching Legal and Factual Research

The presentation skills module of the Westfields Conference on Teaching Legal and Factual Research in Law Firms approaches the subject from a training point of view. The goal of the module is to prepare attendees to:

1. Recognize the difference between teaching and training.
2. Conduct a gap analysis of their own presentation skills.
3. Apply adult learning principles to build their skills.
4. Discover their own style of humor.
5. Use the lecture method effectively.
6. Identify the critical components of training programs.

The materials in this handbook are intended to support these goals and to provide you with a training gestalt.

The materials consist of:

- Differences Between Speakers and Trainers
- Presentation Skills Bibliography
- Andragogy in Action
- Trainer/Trainee Readiness Grid
- Seating Arrangements
- Audio Visuals
- Handout Architecture
- Presentation Checklist
- *Information Anxiety* Quotes

Speakers and Trainers

PRESENTER:	PLATFORM SPEAKER	SEMINAR TRAINER
Purpose:	Inform Persuade Entertain	Change participant's behavior through interactions
Style:	One-way communication	Two-way communication
Method:	Tells them what he's going to tell them Tells them Tells them what he's told them	Determines what they already know Determines what they need to know Fills in the gaps
Tools:	Humor Anecdotes Vocabulary	Lectures Role-plays Exercises Case Studies Demonstrations Visual Aids Questions
Evaluation:	Applause	Behavioral change

Differences Between Speakers and Trainers

The **purpose** of a speaker is to inform, persuade or entertain. It's one–way communication: the speaker speaks, the audience listens. The trainer, however, uses two–way communication to ensure that everyone is involved in the learning process. A trainer provides information for the audience to actively participate in the program.

To create a learning environment, the trainer spends only 30% of the time lecturing; the remainder of the time is used in applying the material and interacting with participants.

Thus, the process of training differs from speaking as well. Instead of talking to the audience, a trainer talks with the audience, asking them what they know. A trainer compares that to what they need to know, then fills in the missing information.

The speaker uses humor and anecdotes as the primary tools for an effective presentation. The trainer uses these tools, too, but also others: lectures, role–plays, exercises, case studies and demonstrations.

The final difference between a speaker and a trainer lies in feedback on the presentation. A speaker receives immediate feedback through applause. A trainer receives feedback through written evaluations from the audience.

Getting Things Started

It's important to start your training session properly. Make sure that participants are relaxed and comfortable, and that the learning environment is positive. You can do this by:

1. Establishing rapport

Begin creating a comfortable learning environment as soon as participants enter the room. The following can help you:

- Smile and show enthusiasm. Greet participants as they arrive, and chat with them. This will put them at ease.

- Establish credibility and identification early in the session. Introduce yourself and explain why you are qualified to lead the session.
- Maintain eye contact with participants. Periodically look directly at each participant.
- Use humor. Laughter aids in establishing an informal friendly atmosphere.
- Walk toward the group and around the room as you speak. Also, during exercises, walk around to check learners' progress.

2. *Using "icebreakers" to get participants involved*

Establish your role as trainer rather than lecturer early in the program. If you don't involve people in a participative exercise within the first 20 minutes, they resort to the conditioning they received as schoolchildren. They become passive and are less apt to share experiences and get involved in the learning process. An "icebreaker" exercise conducted at the beginning of the session helps you build a friendly, informal atmosphere by allowing the participants to become acquainted with one another and with you. A good icebreaker:

- Is brief (a one–hour session would have a five– to 10–minute icebreaker).
- Relates to the seminar topic.
- Helps people associate their experiences with the subject matter.
- Is creative.
- Involves all participants in a non–threatening activity such as performing a task, solving a problem, answering a question or discussing an issue.

Training Model

Do a gap analysis to determine training objectives

↓

Create a lesson plan based on adult learning theory

↓

Choose training methods

↓

Apply facilitative techniques

↓

Evaluate the program

Gap Analysis

The first step in developing a successful training program is to determine participants' training needs. You must identify what participants should be doing and what they actually are doing now. Determining the gap between their current skill level and the required skill level is called a "gap analysis." A gap analysis can be done with a survey, personal observation, an interview or a combination of these.

Setting Objectives

When you have determined the deficiencies in performance, or conducted a "gap analysis," you have arrived at what the participants need to know. Next, you formalize these training needs into training objectives. What exactly is an objective and how do you write a clear one? An objective is a statement of what learners will be able to do at the end of a training program. It describes a learning need and is written from the participants' viewpoint. An objective must be clearly stated and action-oriented. It must:

1. Describe an action the trainee will perform.
("You will be able to...")
2. Be specific and detailed.
3. Be attainable/realistic.

Create a Lesson Plan

Your role as trainer differs from that of school teacher. Adults assimilate information differently from children. Children are taught what is considered important — reading, writing, and arithmetic. On the other hand, adults decide for themselves the importance of material based on its usefulness and relevance. Children don't challenge the information that is presented, but adults do. Most importantly, children can't serve as an information resource for the trainer and participants. Adults have a wealth of knowledge and experience that others may find helpful. In a good training program, trainers take advantage of the valuable resources and shared experiences that adults can provide.

Adult Learning Theory

Dr. Malcolm Knowles, a well–known authority in adult learning theory, has developed several principles about adult learning, four of which we will cover today. It's important to integrate these principles into your program design.

1. *Adults must be involved in the planning process and be able to relate the learning to their goals.*

Adult learners are more self–directed than their young counterparts. As children, we were conditioned to be dependent, sitting quietly in our seats while the teacher conducted the lesson. As adults, however, we want to be more involved in the learning process. That's why it's important for the trainer to solicit participants' reasons for attending the training program at the beginning, so the program objectives can be adjusted accordingly. This creates a captive audience. After all, you're giving them what they asked for.

2. *Material must be related to the participants' experiences.*

Blend the content of the program with the background and experience of your participants. Make use of their experience by involving them in discussions and exercises. The benefit is that participants often can contribute personal anecdotes and tips that the trainer may not have considered.

3. *Adults are motivated to learn when they identify a need to learn.*

That's why it's important to have the participants assess the gaps between what they can do now and what they want, and need, to do. Once this need is established, participants are motivated to learn.

4. *Adults want practical answers for today's problems.*

When presenting material make sure it's relevant to the learners' daily tasks or problems. Emphasize how the learning can be applied. If the material presented is too theoretical, participants will have difficulty understanding its application to their personal situations.

The Lesson Plan

After selecting program objectives, it's necessary to place them in a logical sequence, or lesson plan. The lesson plan serves as an outline for the program content. Like a speech, a well-constructed outline gives you self-confidence and helps you to stay on track and achieve your objectives. By closely following your plan, you will have time to cover all of your material and review it, too.

Training Methods

Of the several training methods available, role-play, exercise, case study and demonstration, we will cover only today: lecture.

Lecture

As the name implies, the lecture is a prepared talk. It is the most used and abused technique in the training field. It's easy to abuse the lecture technique by talking too long, resulting in a loss of participation and feedback from the group. Yet despite this method's drawbacks, it's effective if you must cover a large amount of material in a short time.

Following are some suggestions to make it more effective and interactive:

If You Must Lecture...

When you must lecture, don't forget to use your acquired public speaking skills. "Tell them what you are going to tell them, tell it to them, then tell them what you have just told them." By rephrasing main points, you ensure retention of material.

To make your lecture more interesting, abandon the lectern and don't read from a script. Personalize your talk by using stories and anecdotes to illustrate your points. Don't forget to also include practical "how to" material. When lecturing:

- *Lecture no longer than 15 minutes before introducing an interactive exercise.* Limit the lecture to six major points or else participants' attention will wander.
- *Use visuals to serve as memory joggers.*
- *Don't overload* the person with information. Address a limited number of "critical behaviors." If a participant continues to do five things that you are trying to discourage, don't address all five. Instead, select one or two things on which the person should focus.
- *Be specific and factual.* Refer to specific behaviors to which you are reacting, e.g., "when you frowned I felt anxious."

- *Respond immediately after the event.* Feedback is most useful if you don't delay your response.
- *Be tactful.* Stress the positive as well as the negative.
- *Be clear.* Have the participant restate your feedback comments, to assure that he/she clearly understood what you said.

Effective Use of Visual Aids

Research shows that 83% of all we learn is through sight. Specifically, research indicates that trainees generally remember 20% of what they hear, 50% of what they hear and see, and 70% of what they hear, see, *and* do.

Presentation Skills Bibliography

I. Join a group or association.

American Society of Training and Development
1630 Duke Street
P.O. Box 1443
Alexandria, VA 12313
(703) 683–8100

ASTD Information Center
Will send bibliographies on specific subjects.

Publishes:
Training and Development Journal ($60)
Training & Development Literature Index ($45)

Holds Annual Conference; has 147 local groups.

Toastmaster's International
P.O. Box 10400
2200 N. Grand Ave.
Santa Ana, CA 92711
(714) 542–6793

Toastmaster's is an excellent way to obtain structured speech/leadership experience at regular intervals in a non–threatening atmosphere. There are over 6,700 chapters. Chapter size is usually relatively small. Costs are low. Membership includes the monthly *Toastmaster* magazine, which contains very practical articles. This magazine is not included in periodical indexes.

American Management Association
135 West 50th Street
New York, NY 10020
(212) 586–8100

Trainer's Workshop bimonthly magazine for professional trainers.

Variety of training seminars in different cities.

II. There are many books and articles. This is a very selective sampling.

Andragogy in Action: Applying Modern Principles of Adult Learning by Malcolm S. Knowles and Associates. Jossey–Bass Inc., San Francisco, 1984.

Malcolm Knowles is the father of adult education theory. Other books can be found in libraries by using the LC headings:

Adult education
Continuing education
Professional education

Information Anxiety by Richard Saul Wurman, Doubleday, 1989. $19.95.

A recent best seller, which should be on everyone's reference shelf. It may change the linear way books are written. One reviewer noted, "one of the great information crafters gives sound counsel on how to craft your own damn information."

"Become a State–of–the–Art Presenter" in 41 *Training and Development Journal*, no. 1, p. 19, Jan. 1987.

Beginning or inexperienced presenters should know that excellence really comes down to a little bit of audience analysis, some knowledge of techniques and a lot of common sense people skills.

"Enhancing HRD with Contract Learning" in 41 *Training and Development Journal*, no. 3, p. 62, Mar. 1987.

An expert in the field of adult learning shares some of his experiences with the hope that others will adopt this cooperative method of teaching.

"Questioning: The Epitome of the Art" in 42 *Training and Development Journal*, no. 1, p. 46, Jan. 1988.

Learn to focus on the question and the answer instead of the answer and the questioner.

"Technology–Assisted Adult Learning" in 41 *Training and Development Journal*, no. 6, p. 98, June 1987.

This three–year research alliance could be a model for other business–education ventures. The changing nature of information and the number of people needing access to it require a shift in focus from the information to the learning process itself.

"The Nonprofessional Trainer" in 43 *Training and Development Journal*, no. 10, p.19, Oct. 1989.

Four trainers offer advice to the sometime trainer.

"Training Foreigners" in 42 *Training and Development Journal*, no. 11, p. 81, Nov. 1988.

Author is a cross–cultural communications specialist who writes about training problems resulting from cultural misunderstandings.

"Training 101: Arranging the Training Room — and the Trainer" in 43 *Training and Development Journal*, no. 3, p. 19, Apr. 1989.

Practical guidelines for arranging the physical training facilities.

"Cracking the Communications Ice" in 43 *Training and Development Journal*, no. 4, p. 56, Apr. 1989.

> *Describes an ice breaker which opens channels of communication by identifying behavioral styles of the seminar participants.*

"You Can't Write a Speech" in 41 *Training and Development Journal*, no. 4, p. 70 Apr. 1987.

> *A step–by–step process that makes public speaking come alive.*

"Trainers or Trainees–Who Dominates? in 41 *Training and Development Journal*, no. 5, p. 64, May 1987.

> *No training style works well in every situation. Some trainees need lots of guidance, while others need very little. The trick is determining which group your are dealing with.*

"Malcolm" in 43 *Training and Development Journal*, no. 10, p. 38, Oct. 1989.

> *Excerpts from Knowle's new book The Making of an Adult Educator. Three qualities of the effective helper:*
>
> *Unqualified positive guard for the helpee*
> *A deep ability to empathize*
> *Authenticity — to behave out of your real personhood rather than out of some role.*

"Color Me Training" in 38 *Training and Development Journal*, no. 3, p. 42, Mar. 1984.

> *Explains how learners react to color and the best colors to use for training facilities.*

"Peer Influence and Learning" in 42 *Training and Development Journal*. no. 6, p. 50, June 1988.

> *Participants engaged in moderate levels of peer interaction perform significantly better than those without any peer interaction.*

"Teachers and Trainers: Strategies from the Third Grade" in 41 *Training and Development Journal*, no. 9, p. 68, Sept. 1987.

> *Many educators with experience in both settings realize that the worlds of teaching and training have a great deal in common.*

"Executive Transformation Programs" in 42 *Journal of Training and Development Journal*, no. 12, p. 32, Dec. 1988.

> *Article concentrates on executive training but attorney could be substituted for executive throughout this article for law applications. Has a good summary of the principles and practices of adult learning.*

"Making Trainees Want to Learn" in 42 *Training and Development Journal*, no. 6, p. 43, June 1988.

> *Unless you get and keep learners' attention, you are wasting everyone's time.*

"Library Instruction in the Private Law Firm Environment" in 5 *Legal Reference Services Quarterly*, Summer/Fall 1985.

> *Re–reading this classic article is an interesting exercise after reading some of the adult education/training literature. The problems identified in teaching legal research in law firms are the same as for organizing training programs in any setting.*

III. Reference Tools.

Effective Training Techniques. American Management Association. 60–minute video. Order from Films Inc. (800) 323–4222. Shows trainers how to "break the ice" and generate involvement among trainees.

The Encyclopedia of Icebreakers. University Associates, Inc., 8517 Production Avenue, San Diego, CA 9212 (619) 578–5900, $69.95 for 1988 edition.

> *A looseleaf sourcebook of 150 warm–up designs for use in workshops and training programs. The work is divided into categories*

such as energizers, feedback games, openers, getting acquainted, and professional development topics.

The Encyclopedia of Group Activities: 150 Practical Designs for Successful Facilitating. University Associates, Inc., 8517 Production Avenue, San Diego, CA 92121 (619) 578–5900, $89 for 1989 edition.

A looseleaf handbook of activities categorized according to emphasis. Category divisions include personal awareness, values clarification, communication, group process, feedback and miscellaneous. Designs for facilitator range from very simple to complex. Each exercise describes goals, appropriate group size, activity time required, materials, physical setting process and possible variations of the activity.

From Speaker to Trainer. Toastmasters International, P. O Box 10400, 2200 N. Grand Ave., Santa Ana, CA 92711 (714) 542–6793. $45.

A program module designed to help you move from being a speaker to an effective trainer. This program takes about 4–1/2 hours to present. Included in this program are preparation guidelines, instructions on how to present the program and a complete scan/outline, including group exercises and overhead transparencies. This program is flexible. You can tailor the agenda to meet the needs of the group and the requirements of your schedule.

Training and Development Organizations Directory. Gale Research (313) 961–2242. Updated by supplement. $295 for 4th ed. 1988

A directory of firms, institutes, specialized university programs and other agencies which offer training for managerial, professional and technical personnel. The fourth edition lists over 2,300 such agencies. Descriptive information is provided by the program sponsor. The 5th edition is scheduled for publication in 1991.

Andragogy in Action: Applying Modern Principles of Adult Learning by Malcolm Knowles, published by Jossey–Bosse, San Francisco, Washington and London 1984 was not available for this publication. Check with the publisher for a copy in your area.

Assessing Readiness

Define "trainer readiness" as "the trainer's confidence and competence to conduct this particular session."

Some of the variables that affect a trainer's readiness:

- How many times the trainer has taught the information before.
- The amount of knowledge the trainer has.
- How much preparation the trainer has done.
- The rapport between the participants and the trainer before the class begins.

Some of the variables that affect trainees' readiness:

- Their supervisors' perception of the training.
- Their need for the information or skill provided.
- The relationship of this information or these skills to promotions.
- What they have heard about the training class from previous participants.

The Readiness Grid

Quadrant 1	Quadrant 2
Quadrant 3	Quadrant 4

High ——————— Trainee Readiness ——————— Low

Training Room Arrangement 1: Classroom style

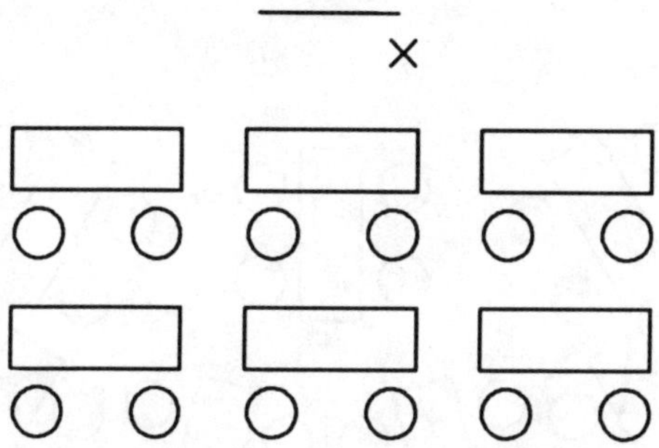

Training Room Arrangement 2: U–Shaped

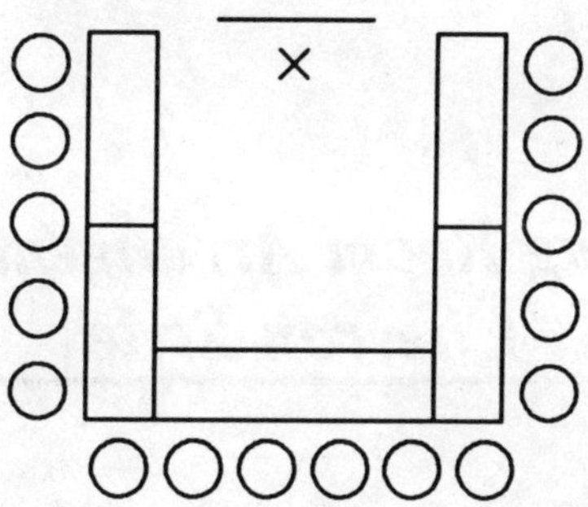

Training Room Arrangement 3: Boardroom

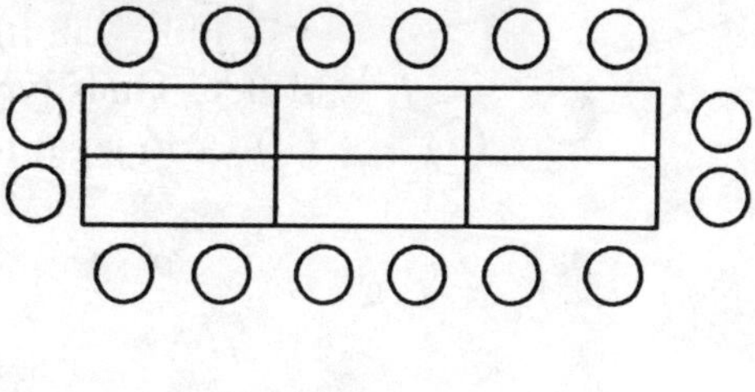

Training Room Arrangement 4: Cluster Style

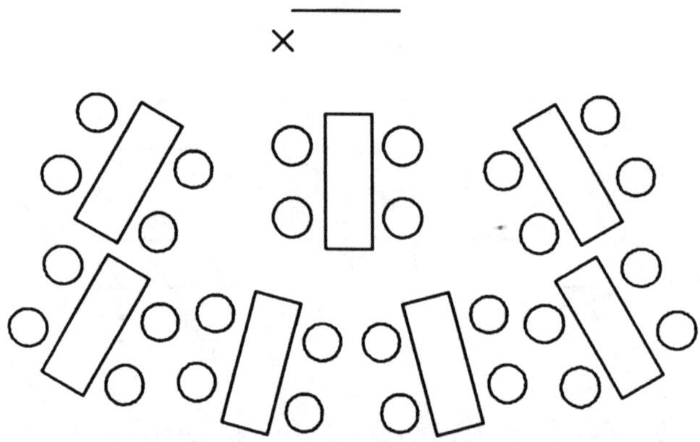

Training Room Arrangement 5: Chevron Style

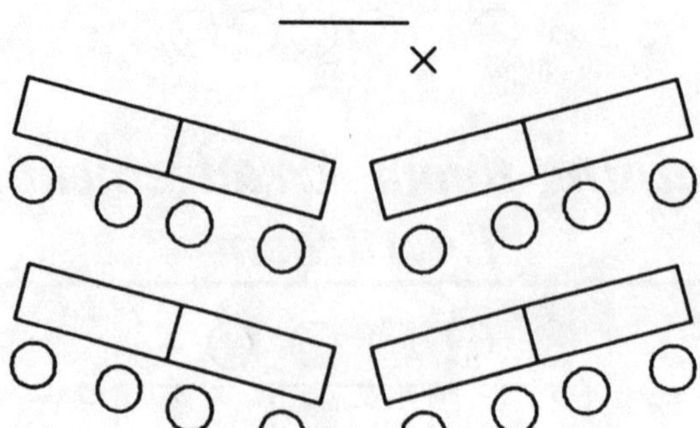

Effective Use of Visual Aids

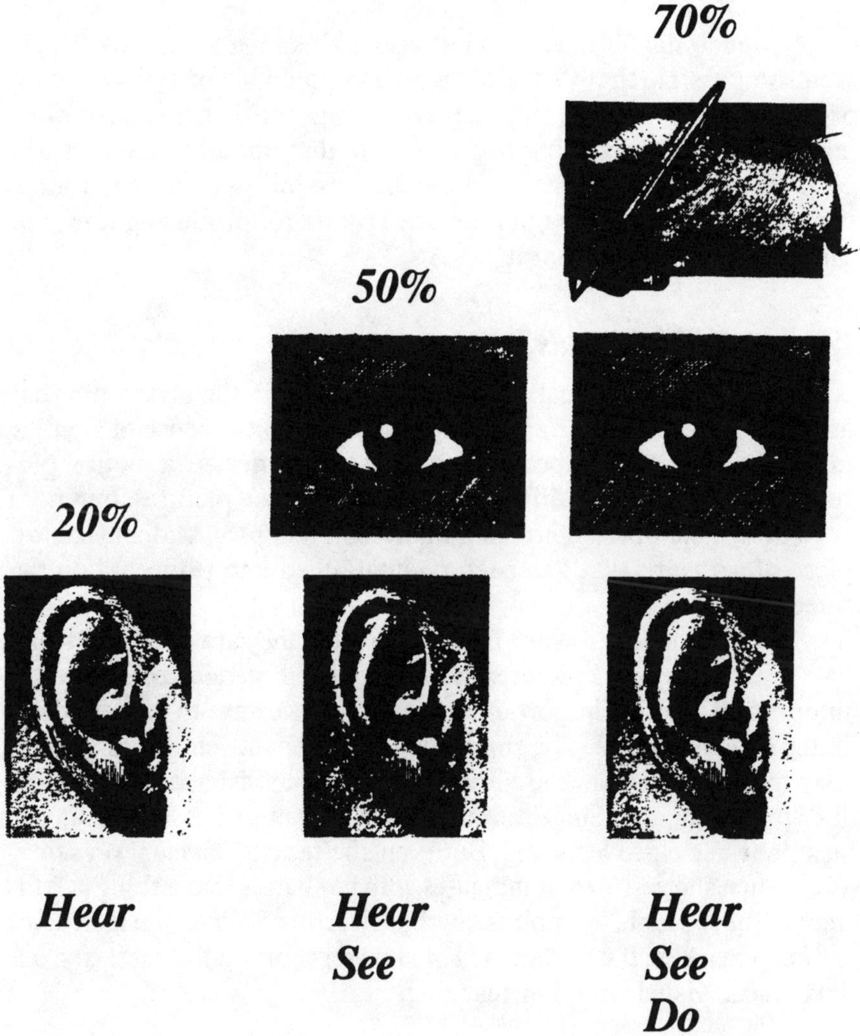

Visual Aids

So much has been said about visual aids in recent years that it seems impossible that they are not an accepted part of every training program. Unfortunately, only lip service is given to them in many training situations. But it is important to note that not all visual aids are good visual aids. Besides the practical, useful, well-designed aids, there are those which do not meet any criteria for producing learning. They may, in fact, prevent it.

What Are Visual Aids?

Very simply, a visual aid is anything used in the classroom that attempts to teach by showing or by appealing to the sense of sight. It may be a chart, a chalkboard, a demonstration device, a motion picture or any one of many different kinds of projected pictures. It may be something held in the hand, or a many-colored, professionally drawn piece of art work that has been photographed and projected on the screen.

Why define visual aids? Because so often they are put into a small category of projected pictures, and either used or rejected. To better understand why it is important to use visuals, we have to think of them in the broadest sense. The supervisor who gets a teaching assignment may try to soothe her conscience by saying that visual aids belong to the "professionals." Since the supervisor is a nonprofessional, she will just limit herself to lecturing. But even she resorts to visual presentations when she gestures or indicates with her hands that a thing is "this shape," or "so high," or points "in this direction." When the instructor makes a mark on the chalkboard or shows a chart on the easel, she has introduced visuals into her teaching.

Reprinted from Martin M. Broadwell, the Supervisor as an Instructor: A Guide for Classroom Instruction, 4th ed.(Reading, Mass.: Addison-Wesley, 1984).

There should be a clear understanding, of course, that it does not necessarily follow that any visual aid is a good aid just because it fits the definition of a visual aid. Some have felt that a picture, even a bad picture, is always worth a thousand words. So far as bad pictures are concerned, even a few good words are often better. So it is as much a failing to use bad pictures in training as it is not to use pictures at all.

Preparing Visual Aids

There are a number of things to consider when we start to prepare visual aids, but time will allow us to look at only the more basic considerations. We'll look at some rules which give us an insight into how visual aids can be produced simply but effectively. First, let's look again at the words "Visual Aids." The description says it is an aid, not something that will do all the teaching for us. The description also says that what we produce should be of a visual nature, at least implying that it should be a picture or visualization of something. Putting it another way, a visual aid is something that aids the student and the teacher in the teaching–learning activity by presenting something that can be seen, because seeing it will be a more effective way to learn than hearing, touching, smelling or tasting it. With this thought in mind, we can now look at the basic rules for preparing visuals and understand why we're planning to use them in the first place.

1. **Visuals should be horizontal**. Most screens are horizontal, and this allows full use of the screen. It also allows for projection over the heads of the students.

2. **Material should be proportional to the frame**. For maximum size, design the original to make use of all the frame — horizontally designed,horizontally photographed, horizontally projected.

3. **Use color for a purpose**. Color should be used, but only because there is a message that can be transmitted better with color. Visuals should teach, not win art contests!

4. **Avoid over–illustrating**. Make the visual single–purposed where possible. One message, one visual, is a good rule.

5. **Orient the viewer**. Whether with arrows, colors, or words, let the viewer know immediately what to look at and where it is on the screen.

6. **Use visuals in moderation.** Limit the visuals not only to the message, but also to the students' endurance time. Go to another format to break up the monotony of too many visuals.

7. **Know the purpose of the visual.** In designing or selecting a visual ask, "Why am I using a visual at all?" The answer should tell if the one we pick is the right one.

Perhaps it's worthy of note here that in many organizations, the visuals are prepared, if not designed, by people in the graphic arts department of the operation. This means that they are most likely interested in producing a quality product by their standards. Their training is not in producing learning, but in producing attractive visuals; and for this reason we may find that though the visual is beautiful, it violates the rules described above. This suggests that we had better not give them just an idea and let them have free rein with color, design, layout, content, etc. They may not understand or even like our idea, especially the simplicity of it, and in order to prepare the visual properly they need a good explanation of its learning goals. An even better solution is to have them attend a session of our regular instructor training program that is devoted to how people learn.

Which Visual Aid to Use?

There seems to be a perpetual argument over which kind of visual aid is best. Some discount the chalkboard, others have no use for overhead projectors and some belittle the slide projector. What it all amounts to is that all kinds of visuals have their place and each has its own strengths and weaknesses.

The best visual to use is the one that will best produce the learning desired within the limitations of the classroom, available equipment, preparation time and budget. Often the instructor has no choice, because the type of visual to be used has already been determined by the equipment in the classroom. Entire books have been written on the subject of visual aids, and so no effort will be made here to discuss the advantages and disadvantages of every kind of projector and technique. Rather, we will consider some of the more common classroom devices, and what the instructor should hope to accomplish with each.

Projection Equipment

Motion Pictures

The motion picture, as has already been pointed out, is excellent both as a training tool and attention getter. Supervisors who come to the classroom as teachers are limited to "shelf" films, since they aren't likely to have the budget, time or experience to make movies just for their use. There are many good firms available on a variety of subjects, however, and these should be given careful consideration. Most industries have their own libraries of films which either are made by them or deal with subjects relating to their activities. This would be a natural place for the instructor to look first. In addition, most companies also have catalogs of available films, and the instructor may find suitable films that can be borrowed from other industries. Even if a film does not exactly fit in every case, the instructor may still be able to use it, explaining that "certain procedures are obsolete, or are done differently in our company." Unless the film contributes so little that it is a waste of time, the trainees would generally prefer to see it anyway. There are certain operations which almost have to be shown in motion to be understood. For this, there is no substitute for a film.

Slide Projection

For compact storage and ease of operation, perhaps nothing is as effective as the slide projector. It also, like motion pictures, allows the use of color. Equipment now available in almost every training location allows for showing large numbers of slides by remote operation. The slides can be sorted, changed, replaced, and substituted in a matter of moments. A presentation can be stored in the same cartridge that is used for projecting, so the instructor has merely to pick out the container for a particular subject, and the visuals are ready to go. Since most projectors change the slides almost instantly, the instructor can even build a sequence easily and effectively, with each slide adding a subsequent step. The instructor can use color to help the build up, and with remote control at a fingertip, does not have to break the presentation to go to the next slide. The movement attracts the student's interest, and well-prepared slides help to hold it. The same remote control may even allow for reversing the slides to return to an earlier one if there are questions. The teacher can stand up at the front, use a pointer if necessary, and easily keep control of the group.

For all the advantages, slide projection has several drawbacks, and the trainer should be aware of these before using slides.

One disadvantage is the necessity for having the room in almost total darkness. If any extraneous light shines on the screen, much of the color will be lost to the audience. Any time lights are turned off in a classroom, there is the danger of losing some of the students through drowsiness or inattention. This is particularly true if the instructor spends too much time on one slide. Where commercial services are used, slides have the disadvantage of being rather expensive, especially for one–time use. Commercial art work is also expensive, especially if the slide is to be on the screen for just a matter of seconds. When these services are available through internal sources, the cost to the company is considerably reduced. Time is also a prime consideration, although most cities now are able to provide one or two–day service in producing slides.

The problem of light in the classroom can be remedied somewhat by having a light in the rear of the room, or directing a light against the wall or ceiling. This will provide enough light to let the students refer to written material and take notes, if necessary. This may also be of help to teachers, since they may need a source of light to read their own notes.

Filmstrips

Filmstrips, or series of continuous still shots on single rolls of film, are also easy to store and use. It's possible to have a roll of over a hundred frames in one small can, making storing and carrying very easy. Since there is no cutting or mounting to be done, the production is quite reasonable, too. Once there is a master negative, reproducing the filmstrips is a simple matter. Laboratories will usually print, box and label for you at very reasonable rates, and you get a roll of film that's ready to project. The filmstrip projector can be one with automatic advance — triggered by sound messages sent from a tape or record narration — or can be manually operated. As in the slide production, it is possible to have an audible tone to signal the operator when its time to change the frame. The change can be from a remote control, push-button switch or manual operation at the machine. The automatic advance, with an inaudible signal, is so rapid that the viewer rarely sees the motion between frames.

There is a disadvantage, though, in the production of filmstrips. Since there must be a continuous film, the negative should be shot as a continuous entity, too. When shooting 75 to 100 shots, it's easy to forget one, to miss an overlay, or get one out of sequence. When this happens, the negative will be incorrect, and it is costly to produce a filmstrip from the two or three negatives required to correct the problem. Another disadvantage is that once the program is put together, it's not wise to splice in new shots. Not many projectors will take the spliced film. It's usually advisable to reshoot a new negative for each change, meaning an additional expense. The old film is no longer of value, since it really isn't profitable to try to use it in anyway.

Overhead Projectors: Transparencies

Overhead projectors, so called because the lens is on a stand over the item to be projected, offer a versatility which combines some of the features of the chalkboard with some of the advantages of the slide projector. One big advantage is that the room light can be left on (although light must not shine directly on the screen). This is a decided help to instructors, since they do not have to bother turning lights off and on. Also, going suddenly from a dark room to a bright one is slightly irritating to the students, and the overhead projector eliminates this problem.

When transparencies are shown on the overhead projector, trainers can write on the picture, cover up certain parts of it, and/or point with a pencil to whatever parts they wish, without going to the screen. The projector is designed with a wide-angle lens so it can be used close to the front of the room, near the instructor. Some instructors prefer to sit beside the machine and teach from this position. This is generally the best arrangement, since it allows the students to see and enables the instructor to change his or her own transparencies. (Pictures in the overhead projector cannot be changed by remote control.)

With the proper equipment, overhead transparencies can be made in a matter of seconds, even from printed sheets or classroom notes. Some equipment even includes color in this quick process. Longer processes allow for more liberal use of color. Even photographs can be made into transparencies with the right developing processes. The overhead projector has some disadvantages, as has been mentioned. One decided disadvantage is that it allows itself to be misused easily. When correctly used, it is very effective, but when misused, it is the least effective of all visual aids. For example, it is easy to simply reproduce whole letter-sized sheets in black and white; it can be done in a few seconds. But the result is often a very unsatisfactory, unexciting and ineffective visual. Some instructors try to enhance such transparencies by covering up all but the line being discussed, and moving down the page a line at a time. This can be effective, sometimes, but it can also be tedious to the instructor and monotonous to the student, especially if the material is barely readable to begin with!

Another drawback is the necessity of having to be close to the equipment much of the time to change transparencies. Instructors lose their ability to move about and keep up interest with their movement. Also, sitting and teaching is an easy way to kill the enthusiasm of both the student and instructor. An experienced instructor can carry on a successful teaching session, but a supervisor coming from the job should not try to teach from a sitting position for very long. One caution: No member of the group should ever be asked to give up his or her opportunity to learn in order to change the transparencies for the instructor.

Video

The use of video has grown and improved rapidly in the last few years. It provides an immediate viewing of something that has just been filmed. Unlike the movie, there is no waiting time for developing, processing and reproducing. Just as in the audiotape, videotape can be rewound and played back almost instantly. Like the movie, video is ideal for showing motion or for showing things that need to be studied from a visual, rather than an audible, standpoint. It takes only a little practice to get fairly proficient at using the equipment, and most of the tapes are now in cartridges of some kind, so storage is easy, though not inexpensive. The quality of the end product is good in both color and black and white. Since most of us live in a "TV" world, students find little difficulty in looking at programs in that format. It's now possible to project to full-sized screens, if we have the equipment, so there isn't the problem of multiple monitors.

As good as it is, there is still misuse of video as a medium. Often it is used where sound would be all that is needed to do the teaching. In an interview, for instance, where we're trying to teach a sequence of questions, and are not concerned about body language, video has a serious drawback. Since sight is usually more attention getting than sound, the replay of the interview on video may cause the students to get more involved in looking than in listening.

Cost is still a factor to be reckoned with, though it is much lower and the quality much better, than a few years ago. Compatibility from one machine to the next is no longer much of a problem, and the limitation on the use of the equipment after it has been purchased is no longer cost but imagination.

Chalkboard

Nothing is more commonly used in the training room than the chalkboard, yet it is probably misused as often as it is used correctly. Why? Because, like the overhead projector, it lends itself to misuse. The teacher has to develop good chalkboard habits and then consciously use them.

The chalkboard is an excellent teaching aid, the teacher's real standby in any crisis. A diagram, a crude picture, a rough sketch can often help students who are uncertain of an idea to understand it quickly. The instructor can trace out the solution of a problem for a befuddled trainee in moments, then erase it and be ready for the next item of discussion. The instructor can place complex diagrams on the board, piece-by-piece, as the student easily follows each step. Where further explanation is needed, the instructor can add to an explanation or make changes with very little effort. Colored chalk can be used to show various components.

But all of this versatility is not without handicaps. The chalkboard is an open invitation for the trainers to violate almost all good training techniques. First, they can talk to the board instead of the group, thus losing eye contact and possibly cutting down their volume to the point where the people in the back row can't hear. In talking to the board, they may cover up what is written, so the students can't see it. Then their writing may be so small — or so poor — that no one can read it. What really frustrates trainees who are having to copy down long lists or other information from the board is to have instructors erase the material when they are halfway through and casually say, "You won't need to write this down; I have copies for you."

The Easel

The paper easel or flip chart differs from the chalkboard in that information can be put on ahead of time and covered up, then it can be saved by merely turning the page. All the things said about the misuse of the chalkboard apply as well to the easel. Charts can be enlarged to easel size and placed in with the paper for handy reference. Caution should be taken, however, to see that the original chart (or copy to be enlarged) is readable. If the original isn't legible, the enlarged one may not be much better. By touching up the original the result can be improved, and touching up the enlargement will help even more. Color can be added to the enlarged copy to help bring out important points. The color should be meaningful, though, and should never be used just to have color. Misuse of color can emphasize an unimportant point, letting a significant fact or idea be lost because it is not in color. As with all visuals, the material on the easel should be large enough to be seen and simple enough to be understood.

Before Application of Stylesheets — Text and Graphic Parts

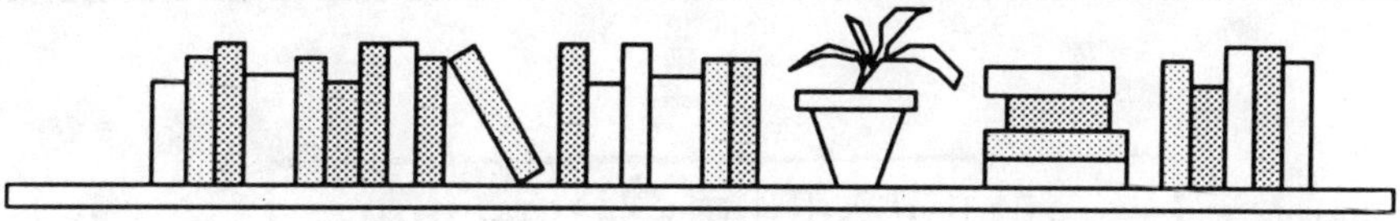

Broken Quill Award

Applicant is employed by a car dealership. He does no manual-type work, no mechanical work, no delivery work, and no sales. He is the manager.

– *Report by insurance investigator*

Audience

If you really want to help the American theater, don't be an actress, darling. Be an audience.

– *Tallulah Bankhead*

In Hollywood the woods are full of people that learned to write but evidently can't read. If they could read their stuff, they'd stop writing.

– *Will Rogers*

The only unchanging rule in technical communication is that the audience is always right.

– *R. John Brockmann*

The Final Composed and Printed Page

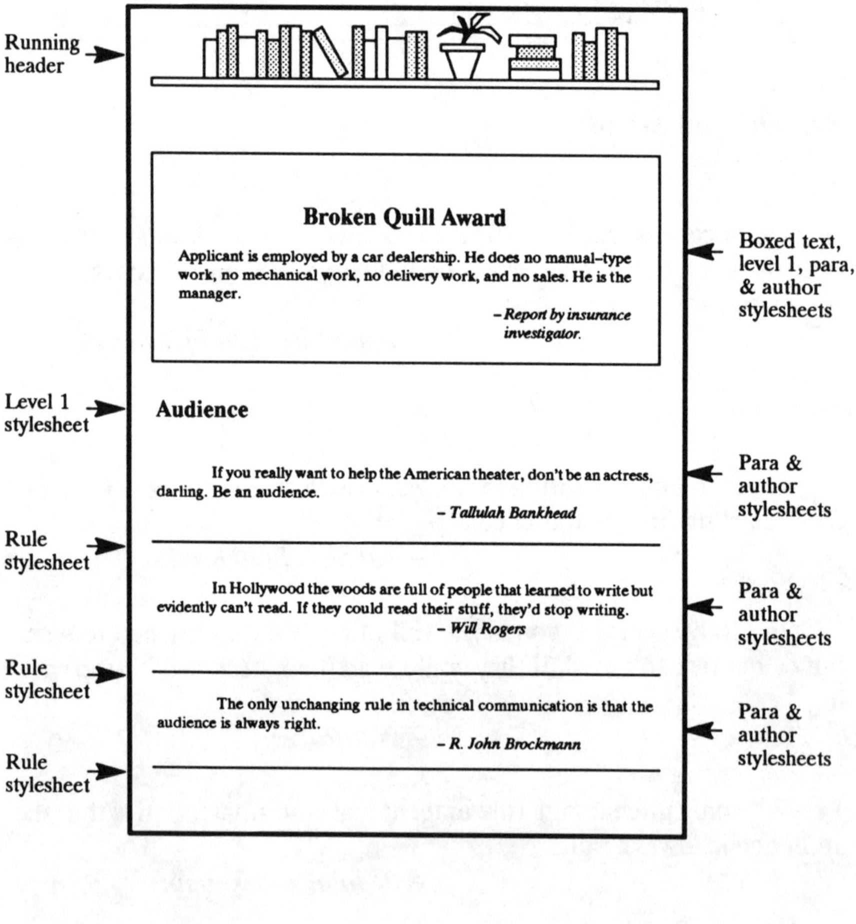

Variable Thresholds or "Tolerance Levels"

From an Information Theory point of view, humans have physiological tolerance levels or thresholds for information (Miller, 1981; Pearson, 1967; Shannon, 1960). But these levels are determined by the structure of information rather than solely by its quantity. For example, even though the tones, loudness, and texture of noise from a construction site may be similar in quantity to a symphony by Mahler, a listener finds the latter more tolerable and meaningful due to the structure of the sounds. In other words, much of what we see and hear is "noise" from which we actively extract the information we need or want. In this sense, information which is carefully structured before being presented to the senses assists readers in understanding more complex information. In some respects, this relationship between comprehension and structure is implicit in the very nature of information itself, for in philosophical terms, information is structure. Scientists like C.S. Smith (1981) and philosophers like Korzybski have been suggesting this relationship between information, structure and comprehension for many years in remarks like: "The only content of knowledge is structure"(Korzybski, 1936) and "Everything that we can see, everything that we can understand, is related to structure" (Smith, 1981).

Figure 3: Information Overload (based on Miller, 1981)

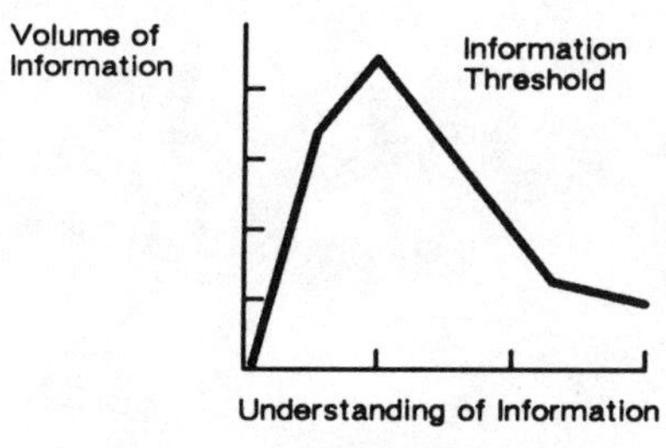

Figure 3 indicates that comprehension and quantity of information arc positively correlated only to a certain point. Beyond that point, excess quantity (or insufficient structure) results in the rapid decline of comprehension. This view of the brain's response to information can be converted into a set of operations which designers can use to structure information into effective, "coherent" messages. In these terms information consists of structures of data, and "understanding" (consists of) a set of processes performed on data structures" (Kosslyn,

1981). Designers who work from this perspective essentially "pre-process" information by structuring it coherently. Five relevant techniques drawn from cognitive science upon which information designers rely are: ***chunking, queuing, filtering, mixing modes and abstracting.*** By using these techniques, designers "pre-process" information in ways which measurably influence a reader's attitude, speed of task performance, error rate and memory.

Figure 4: Five Pre–processing Techniques

Chunking
Zoning or structuring the visual field by breaking information into manageable chunks according to their subject matter and then allocating them to various areas on a surface, screen or page.

Queuing
Ordering chunks of information in a spatial array hierarchically, that is, in an arrangement which suits the end user's sense of subject matter order and importance.

Filtering
Simplifying linguistic and visual order to "filter out" unnecessary "background noise" which interfaces with the information being transmitted. Also, layering information, i.e., creating levels of depth and legibility through the use of visual metaphors, color and tone, or by varying the sizes and weights of type.

Mixing Modes
People learn by using different cognitive modes or styles. Some prefer or need text ("strings"); others need illustrations, photos, diagrams or visual analogs ("images"); others demand formulae and other quantitative materials ("propositions").

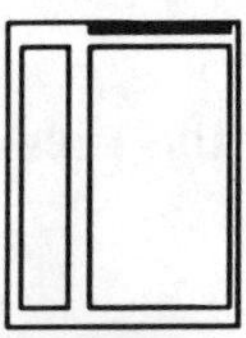

Abstracting
Building effective visual information systems which work consistently over time on various media and in the hands of many users requires graphics systems which are characterized by simplicity, elegance and continuity. As in philosophy and mathematics, truly useful design systems can only be arrived at after considerable "abstraction."

Presentation Checklist

1. What?

What is the focus of your presentation — What you, a law librarian, know or what skills law library users require?

What identified user group(s) lack what cluster of skills?

Can these skills and/or concepts be woven into a topic of interest?

What will you call the presentation? Seminar, training session, conference, workshop, library user support envelope, legal research made easy, life after LEXIS, research survival skills, library lambada, commando legal research, initializing your information software?

Is this a single presentation, the first of a series or a regular event?

What relevant and timely examples can you use for demonstrations?

What does the group already know? Does your presentation build on this base?

Will you be in a teaching or training mode? Which is best for this presentation?

Have you identified specific activities/behaviors that will be changed by the presentation?

What have you done, separate from a presentation, to present the library as a transparent system and to create a visual information gestalt? Signs, posters, maps, pathfinders, newsletters, library guides?

What have you done to engineer usability and information products into the design of your library?

2. *Where ?*

Where is the most suitable place for the presentation? Will this be a seated or walking presentation? Both?

Can you arrange chairs and tables into a user–friendly configuration?

Does the space have the amenities required? Electric outlets, wall for overheads, VCR, chairs, tables, coffee, computers?

Is the space away from interruptions? Does it have a phone for emergency contacts?

Is the space large enough if everyone shows? Will it be too big if only a few persons come? Will it be comfortable for people to drift in and out?

Have you provided a comfortable and relaxed environment (food, beverages, games, puzzles) so that learning takes place easily?

3. *When?*

When during the year is the best time to schedule presentations?

Which day of the week and the month is best to schedule the presentation in light of the pace of your organization?

When might there be conflicts with departmental meetings or other training programs?

What time of the day should the presentation be held?

When should the presentation end? How long should the presentation last?

If a series of presentations are scheduled, what time period is optimal?

4. How?

How will you establish rapport with the audience? How will you use an icebreaker? How will you create a bond between members of the group as well as between you and the group?

How will you use the audience's vocabulary, thinking mode and ideas?

How is the presentation linked to the firm's practice?

Have you provided an agenda/outline of the presentation for each person?

How can you use this agenda/outline to keep your presentation seem relaxed and informal?

How professional are your handouts? Are they packaged to stand alone? Do they have color, texture, rhythm, balance, sufficient white space? Is the information they contain chunked, queued, filtered, mixed and abstracted to avoid information overload and to provide coherent messages?

How varied is your presentation in terms of media? In terms of learning styles? What techniques will you use in addition the lecture method? Questions, exercises, discussion, humor, metaphors, overheads, neon, slides, videos, songs, dance, images, cartoons, diagrams, computers, icons, mascots, posters, mottos, cheat sheets?

How are your ideas organized? Transactionally or bibliographically? Is it clear at the beginning what you are setting out to accomplish? Are your ideas tied together with an over–arching image or theme? Do you have a short, concise, memorable summary at the end?

How will you bring the audience and their information level into the presentation?

Will you be doing a joint presentation with a member of the group, a vendor, another library staff member? If so, how are you planning to integrate the approaches?

How will you provide for feedback?

5. *Who?*

Who have you worked with in the audience to get input on group needs or to identify who needs to know what?

Who have you worked with to sanction your presentation? Have you looped in everyone in the territory?

Who will notify the audience of the presentation? Are you in charge of this or are you relying on someone else?

Who is your back–up in the event you are unable to make the presentation?

Who from the library staff do you want to be present?

Who are you (what role are you playing) when you give the presentation? Team player, facilitator, instructor, maven, agent of change, educator, preacher, librarian, critic, nudge?

Trainers are facilitators.

Giving information is a relatively small portion of their job.

People have a tendency to get hooked into "functional fixedness" or seeing objects only in terms of their conventional uses.

Humor is based on the unconventional and thus can encourage people to transcend this trap.

The computer is an icon for our age, but reason and imagination, which yield understanding are yet to be programmable.

Training equals remembering what it's like not to know.

Take your responsibility seriously, but don't take yourself too seriously.

Trainees are more likely to remember and use what you teach them if they chuckle every time they think about it. Even if they think it's silly at the time, it sticks with them.

Education is to learning as tour groups are to adventure.

In the early stages of acquiring any really new skill, a person must adopt at least a partly anti–pleasure attitude.

Who says, "Good, this is a chance to experience awkwardness and to discover new kinds of mistakes?"